My Untold Stories:
The Roads That Led to Liberation

Brittney Wardlaw, J.D.

My Untold Stories

Copyright © 2024 by Brittney Wardlaw, JD

All rights reserved. No part of this publication may be reproduced, distributed, or transmitted in any form or by any means, including photocopying, recording, or other electronic or mechanical methods, without the prior written permission of the publisher, except in the case of brief quotations embodied in critical reviews and certain other noncommercial uses permitted by copyright law. For permission requests, write to the publisher, addressed "Attention: Permissions Coordinator," at the address below.

Published by:

Brittney Wardlaw

www.therelationshipclinic.com

Produced by:

Create and Blossom

712 Austin Avenue

Waco, TX 76701

www.createandblossomstudios.com

ISBN: 978-1-945304-45-3 hardcover

ISBN: 978-1-945304-85-9 paperback

Library of Congress Cataloging-in-Publication Data

LCCN: Forthcoming

First Edition

Contents

Prologue 5

Introduction: Welcome to Baylor 7

Run Aground Road

    Chapter 1: Truth 13

    Chapter 2: Allies and Friends 17

    Chapter 3: Pet to Threat 36

    Chapter 4: Pushed Out, Burnt Out, or Sell Out ... 49

    Chapter 5: Grief and Loss 58

Reflections Street

    Chapter 6: Insecurity Breeds Oppression 69

    Chapter 7: Sexual Harrassment/Assault v. Racism ... 71

    Chapter 8: Why Don't White Men Bother Me as Much? ... 78

    Chapter 9: ERGs 83

    Chapter 10: $125,000 87

Rehab Drive

    Chapter 11: Control 97

    Chapter 12: The Niggers I've Seen Sold 101

Chapter 13: So What Do You Think of Martin Foster?   107

Chapter 14: When the Two-Step of Their Deception Gets Tangoed   110

Chapter 15: The Day I Felt Molested   117

Recovery Circle

Chapter 16: Light and Dark   127

Chapter 17: A Big 'Thank You'   141

Chapter 18: The Road to Healing and Wholeness   144

Chapter 19: Grief Is a Funny Thing   146

Chapter 20: The Plantation   150

Chapter 21: THE Performance Improvement Plan   154

Chapter 22: Violent White Women   156

Chapter 23: The Casualties   163

Chapter 24: What It Feels Like to Try So Hard and It's Still Not Good Enough   166

Runteldat Way

Chapter 25: Baylor as the Gold Standard   173

Chapter 26: The Big Wins That Meant Nothing   177

Chapter 27: "The Budget"   186

Chapter 28: "Baal-or" University   193

Chapter 29: The Black Woman, Strong   195

Chapter 30: To Sue or Not to Sue   197

Chapter 31: Status and Street Cred	200
Chapter 32: When I Knew It Was Over	203
Chapter 33: Thank You & Farewell	209
Chapter 34: The Two Shall Become One	212
Chapter 35: Elevation with Purpose	216
Chapter 36: Would I Go Back if I Could?	217
Chapter 37: To All of You Who Thought You Knew What You Didn't Know You Thought You Knew	220
Conclusion	223

Appendix

Notes	229
Receipts	249

Endnotes	267

Jesus, He did it.

This book is dedicated to my husband, who has done just what he vowed to do. "To love me as Christ loves Church."

In memory of my grandmother—a strong, wise, and authentic gift to us all.

In memory of my Uncle Linwood, who always encouraged me to speak and write because he said, "You help lead us to freedom just like Harriet did."

Acknowledgements

You may never know how far your words, presence, affirmation, and/or encouragement met me somewhere at a critical point on this journey over the last four years...

Alicia, Murna, Kennisha, Anastacia, Robin, Jasmine, April, Remi, Chanel, Jess, Kara, Morgan, MeQuel, Mary, Jo & Kirk, PJ, DJ, Pastor, Hope & Al, Tonja, Jessica my therapist, my parents, Kim & Ryan, JB, Monica, Britt.

Prologue

Why Kap is on my hero list

I'm inspired by Colin Kaepernick. Watching the *Colin in Black & White* series inspired me because it reminds me of what you can do when you're free. Not enslaved, silenced, or controlled by anyone. You can communicate information and messages that are long overdue in coming to light.

That's exactly why I didn't take the money Baylor University offered me. I've got a story to tell. Many stories, actually, that need to come to light for the liberation and elevation of others. There are many who have been—and are being—elevated and they have no idea the battles fought behind closed doors. The battles that allow them to shine the way they've always deserved to shine. To be honest, there's not a lot of glory in it, but that's OK.

Freedom is the goal. Liberation is the key.

Introduction: Welcome to Baylor

January 2017

I think one of the things that has made beginning to document my journey so daunting is knowing where to begin. As my husband Gary and I talked about my story, he continued to urge me on with his normal "My wife is a Rockstar" urgency. I confessed that I was overwhelmed with the details—*Where do I even start*?

He replied, "The beginning."

The beginning is marked with a complexity of emotions. Hopefulness and great expectation, naivete, wonder, peace, joy—but probably the most clear and unwavering emotion was confidence. Not confidence in myself or the vain pride that would come before a fall. But a pure confidence—much like the one I walked down the aisle with. A confidence that said, "I know this looks crazy and insane and risky and foolish to everyone else, but this is the life I am called and committed to."

I recognize the call deep inside and there's no logic or reason that will deter me from obeying that call. As logical as I am, once the confidence and confirmation of something bigger than myself calls me to the unknown, there's no turning back. That right there is truly *living*. There's no living apart from that—because apart from that is only existing. That confidence—or that *faith*—in which I move. The only faith that can sustain when shit hits the fan. The kind of faith that reminds you of the things you hoped for. The faith that provides proof of the things you cannot see because the rain is too strong, the winds are too ferocious, and the waters are too high.

There will be plenty of people willing and ready to plant the seed that you should have chosen the safe and secure route. You should have chosen the route approved by most. The route that provided predictability.

But that ain't me. That ain't us. *Wardlaws to Waco* was a catalyst and turning point for our family. The kind of faith where you're leaping off a cliff, confident that your parachute will open. You're also just as confident that, even if it doesn't open, God's got a plan on how to catch you. But even if He doesn't catch you, He's got a plan for a soft landing. Even if the landing isn't soft, He's got a plan for recovery. Even if there is no recovery, there's a far greater reward in submission to our obedience. We had a great flight with no regrets.

From the initial breakfast with Kristan, who was my first Baylor supervisor, to the invitation to apply and even to my initial and follow-up interviews, there was an ease and confidence with which I moved. I knew I was responding to a call. It was eerie. In the natural and logical plain, it did not "make sense" to leave my executive-level position at the job of my dreams, at my alma mater. It did not make sense to leave a city filled with my college best friends and siblings—within driving distance from our grandparents—while my husband kicked ass in a Ph.D. program he had always dreamed of. All of this while holding down a full-time position as a therapist in a hospital and a part-time position in a private practice.

We had a church home with a strong black community. We had our one beautiful brown baby in a community with our best friends and their beautiful brown babies who were supposed to grow up together, with babies on the way, in a picturesque suburban neighborhood in our gorgeous new country home in a development on nearly an acre of land. Why leave that? Truly, we were living the American dream at the age of 29 and 27, respectfully.

But faith doesn't make sense. Hardship doesn't feel good. Peace is priceless. Obedience is non-negotiable. So, if we're truly starting from the beginning, that's where the chapters begin...

Part 1:
Run Aground Road

"So keep up your courage, men, for I have faith in God that it will happen just as he told me. Nevertheless, we must run aground on some island." – Acts 27:25-26 NIV

Pictures from September 2018

Chapter 1: Truth

Ever since Gary and I started speaking about our experience with systemic racism, it's caused me to have to not only wrestle but also let go of the comfort of popularity. Now, don't get me wrong, unlike Mr. Wardlaw, I wasn't the most *popular* superlative in school. I didn't have crowds of people enthusiastically respond to memories I had created for others on class trips because of my dynamic and lightning personality!

I'm talking about the simple kind of endearing likeability that merits a warm and enthusiastic welcome when you walk into a room. The kind that gets you invited to the barbecues. The kind that has people waving you down in a parking lot to say hello. Simple likeability that I didn't realize until 2020 was extremely valuable to me and my self-worth.

However, as much as I've always valued and operated in the expectation of being socially embraced, truth and justice have always tipped the scale. But I've managed to have so much acceptance that, even when I choose truth in a moment that can cost some of that popularity, I still have enough not to overly care about the "loss of like." But 2020 and 2021 curbed all of that and ousted me into facing the true weight of truth-telling.

Apparently, there is a very trendy discussion around telling "your truth." I heard someone mention that they didn't like the phrase because it was trendy. I get that. It could be a slippery slope to relativism. But the reality is, when people have a very limited perception of your story, your story quickly becomes "your truth." And as much as you desire your truth to be *the truth*, it may never be accepted as that because of humanity's very limited perspective.

However, at the end of the day, I have a responsibility to tell my story. Free of "gag orders," embellishments, opinions, criticisms, and skeptics. But let's be honest: the critics and skeptics aren't going anywhere, and neither is the truth. Neither is my voice. Neither is my covering.

***

One of the most painful uncertainties in my journey and departure from Baylor University was this gnawing idea of *inadequacy*. Was what they were making me out to be true? Was I not leadership material? Was I not ready to lead? Were my skills and abilities underdeveloped? Was I intellectually and educationally inferior?

To mitigate the potential for blind spots to mislead me, I incessantly self-examined with these questions in mind. Some of the most potent times were when I was denied first-round interview invitations to three different promotional opportunities. Or when COVID hit, and I was the first employee at the entire institution to be moved to a different department under the guise of "resource allocation." Only to be assigned to checking emails with the Texas Hunger Initiative and reporting to a student worker for onboarding.

My greatest disappointment and pains in the denials and demotions were not in economic loss but in the psychological, emotional, and mental erosion of my heart, motivation, and belief in myself... As I watched the series *Amend*,[1] a historical documentary about the evolving and lethal fight for rights in America, and saw the murder of the black mind, body, and soul, I couldn't help but reflect on the attempted murder of *my* mind and soul.

Myself and countless others are made to feel like it is our inadequacies and shortcomings that hinder our progress. And without active, affirmative messages of the opposite, it can take deep root in both the conscious and unconscious mind. After working *under* incompetence for years—as we all have to pretend as if the person in charge is competent—it's degrading to the psyche. We constantly ask ourselves a question that can be answered in only one way—white supremacy[2] and the notion that there is an inherent, God-given superiority bestowed upon the white race that plays in every facet of our society—including education and corporate America. I'm not just talking about myself. I know others have been impacted and continue to work through the effects... countless others.

The very brief Assistant VP of Equity, presumed to be easily controlled, had enough experience to serve as a sufficient placeholder to appease the masses. The university quickly let him go once they discovered that this black man *did* have a mind of his own and would not be manipulated. A dear friend and current Baylor employee who was brilliant, charismatic, and dynamic in every way was hired as a low-level staffer. He quickly established himself, his abilities, and his work ethic on campus. He has served on countless hiring committees for positions of both Provost and President so they could use him for his giftings, intellect, and ability, but then communicate to him that he's not ready to serve in a position of that level—*for almost 15 years.*

Another beautiful black friend—a brilliant marketing mastermind—eventually turned down an opportunity to work overseas. Baylor offered to increase her pay—recognizing her value and their need for her—but not going as far to put her in a position of leadership. This reinforced the unspoken notion and perception that, in spite of the repeated demonstrations of competence, leadership, and influence, these negroes...

I mean, people of color (POC) are not ready to serve in elevated positions of leadership.

Chapter 2: Allies and Friends

"It's not the words of our enemies but the silence of our friends that we remember." – MLK

What are they?

In my training, seminars, and workshops, I've defined an "ally"[3] as one that *takes on the struggle as their own; transfers the benefits of their privilege to those who lack it; amplifies the voices of the oppressed before their own.*

However, my explanations are not limited to these. These are the explanations that are most pertinent to my "friends" at Baylor. And I *have* to use air quotes for these "friends." It's only right. One of the most vivid pictures in my mind of these "friends" was their eyes. As melodramatic as this may sound, I feel as though I spent a lot of time looking into their souls. I was desperate to assess their sincerity at all times. These were the white women that I often turned to for perspective. So I desperately hoped they would give me some insight, perspective, and encouragement to help me navigate this white world that I so desperately sought to be successful in.

They held the keys to the secret doors, the secret mottos, and the secret avenues to acceptance and professional approval. Perhaps the ones discussed at the dinner table in their households, or even the ones shared at the golf course or their child's elitist extracurricular activities. Gary and I once had a friend from Waco that we connected with during our time there. He was brilliant. An Italian born and raised in NYC with a knack for connecting with humanity. We bonded with him because of his Virginia undergraduate education. Difference was, he had attended a very elitist, yet very respected, institution not too far from Liberty.

He said something to the effect of, "Yeah... an Italian New Yorker from a working-class family... it was a total culture shock for me... these guys knew things about how to be successful and retire by 30 that no one in my family had a clue about!"

"Really?!" we exclaimed.

"Yeah... you wouldn't believe it! The things I was learning from them were unwritten and passed down in their homes... attaining the 'American Dream.' It's totally inequitable. That's why I want to package and market [a course] called 'White People Magic.' What do you think?"

What was hilarious but confounding about his question is that he was *deadass.* That conversation we had with him that day was one of the most affirming dispositions I have ever had. For POC in the corporate workplace, particularly in higher education, where my experience lies, some of us often believe we are dogmatic about following directions and instructions to the letter—however, we seem to be missing a page.

Perhaps to both my professional and emotional detriment, I trusted these "friends," or connections to the inside, with the insight I lacked. The truth is, what other choice did I really have? So, whenever shit hit the fan, these "friends" were the shelter I ran to for covering, guidance, and perspective. The way I saw it, I had made significant investments in these relationships, and they were the "jokers" that I brought out on really serious occasions.

***

There was one very vivid and significant occasion that I knew had very real legal and professional ramifications. If there was any time to whip out the "big joker,"[4] it was now.

The Chief of Staff was a white woman from the sociology department. She was appointed over my area of compliance with little to no understanding of any of the specializations of *any* of the departments. It was both a spoken and unspoken understanding that she was absolutely clueless about almost every area, but she would be tasked with its management—ensuring that we all stayed in line and kept her abreast of anything that potentially made her, the President, or the institution look bad.

My brown colleague (who we will call "Sallie") and I were tasked with responding to investigations of any claims of discrimination as it related to protected classes. Sallie had previously been tasked with this responsibility alone for the entire university prior to my transfer to HR. However, neither she nor I had ever found anyone "responsible." I would later come to realize how truly concerning it was to not *ever* find anyone responsible for this type of protected class harassment or discrimination. All of our reports had to be sent to and reviewed by the General Counsel before issuing to any of the parties involved.

If you were to ask Sallie and me, in hindsight, our thoughts on the outcomes of these investigations, I'm not sure I can confidently say we would give the same answer. I'd like to think we would, but I cannot say for sure. Mainly because now that I'm out and can see things with a little more of a focused lens, I understand how heavily influenced and controlled we were by outside entities when it came to conducting a fair and impartial investigation. My colleague relied heavily on the opinion of the General Counsel. Their position, education, and experience held a lot of weight for her. I couldn't blame her. And due to my own insecurities as a trained attorney, I defaulted heavily to their "advice" as well.

We were consistently "advised" that these complaints did not meet the standard of a finding of responsibility of discrimination or harassment—ever. But, an interesting case walked through our door and it was one that we didn't expect to unfold as intricately as it did. We also didn't expect the amount of legwork it required. This particular case was a young black female employee working in the School of Nursing at Baylor's campus in Dallas.

My colleague and I ultimately had to make a couple of trips to the school in order to conduct the investigations in response to her complaint. But, one thing I forgot to mention—her complaint was against the Dean and the Associate Dean of the School of Nursing. Another pair of dear white woman friends who were both being accused of racial harassment and discrimination.

Most of our interviews went well. The complainant's peers were cooperative, shared what they knew, and we were able to do the majority of our fact-gathering. Things got interesting, however, after we were finally able to pin down the Associate Dean for an interview. Every time we tried to schedule, she was on a sabbatical, taking a trip, or not feeling well. It seemed like months before we were finally able to meet with her for an interview.

Ironically, on one of our visits I remember her being the person to greet us at the door, show us around, introduce us to folks, and make sure we were well taken care of. (In retrospect, I'm realizing her hospitality may have been a little over the top.) So when we finally did sit down for an interview with her, I don't think either one of us anticipated the turn it would take.

Now, my colleague and I were pretty pleasant folks, if I do say so myself. I would often joke with her that I was convinced she had to have been Prom Queen, Homecoming Queen, or at least on the court because I had never met someone who didn't think she was one of the most pleasant people ever. Now, I don't purport to be on anyone's homecoming court, but I do know I have a very good read of a room. I do a pretty good job of appealing to an individual's humanity. So, we were a pleasant investigatory duo.

So when this interview went left, it caught us both by surprise. I can confidently say that I don't think we had any different or unique approach to this respondent interview than we did with anyone else we had interviewed in the past. And perhaps, that, in and of itself, was the problem. This individual we sat across from that day had some very clear unspoken expectations that she was to be treated as an Associate Dean and not a "respondent." The reason I know that is because the offense in her responses to our standard questions escalated our interaction *quickly*.

I'm not sure we were in the room longer than 15 minutes before she stormed out, and my colleague and I were left in shock. We sat stunned for a bit and eventually packed up our things and prepared to head back to Waco. As we proceeded down the road, we concluded that we should notify our supervisor, Driskell, and the General Counsel that one of the two respondents refused to continue the interview.

I now have a much clearer understanding of the implications of refusing to participate in an interview with two African American females. Especially where you are being accused of racial harassment and discrimination of an African American female employee who is concerned about the hostile working environment that has been created for her. An environment that she was now on medical leave from because of the impact on her physical, mental, and emotional health.

Nonetheless, we contacted them both as we rode home about the outcome of the interview. We were advised to do what we could with the information that we had. I truly thought the events after these interviews were about to land Baylor in hot water... yet again. This is why I made notes to myself and saved them as evidence that my colleague and I did our best to do the right thing. But we inevitably obeyed the directive of our supervisor with the General Counsel's awareness.

The following week, we met with our supervisor, Driskell, for our usual case review. The focus of our conversation was entirely on the School of Nursing investigation. The only thing I remember about that meeting—and really the only thing that mattered—was that Driskell advised us she had received a call from the Dean of the School of Nursing, and the Dean was "very upset." She had "a lot of concerns about how disruptive Sallie and I were to the working environment at the school." As a result of this conversation, Driskell and the Dean (one of the respondents of this investigation) decided that we should "discontinue the investigation at this time…"

Wait. What? This was not for real. A respondent who likely was a close colleague of my supervisor and my supervisor came to the conclusion that our office would no longer be looking into any more accusations against her or her close colleague, whom she was eventually going to be promoting to Dean. All because they did not like "the disruption" it was causing. Disruption of who and what? Their white comfort? Their fragility, perhaps? My supervisor would later make a similar decision about a black female student accusing a male professor of racial discrimination because he was "really upset."

The whole thing was surreal. It was then that the light bulbs started going off—this role, this office, was a joke. We were simply there to cover their asses and hold space for their fragility. Not to actually do a job. If I had any questions in my mind about the legitimacy of the Equal Employment Opportunity (EEO)[9] office at Baylor University, the questions were answered that day.

At this point in time, I considered one of the members of the General Counsel to be a close colleague and friend. I can't tell you the specifics of our conversation about this advisement. But what I can tell you is that she likely responded the same way she always did with Driskell's questionable directives—with distance and glazed "roboticism." It's truly the only way to explain how I felt when I would desperately seek her brain and heart to engage me in order to help me understand the calls being made around me that were fundamentally wrong on a human level.

Was there anyone with any authority that would see these marginalized bodies disposed of and devoid of their value by discontinuing their investigations? All because several white women in power decided that their pain, their voice, and their marginalization did not matter?

Just another disposable black professional. One that was eventually terminated "for other reasons." Only to have an investigation later "concluded" by my colleague while I was on maternity leave because this nameless black body may have filed an EEO complaint. Oops—guess we have to go ahead and finish this report, so it looks like we did our due diligence as an institution to respond to this disposable black girl's concern.

Was I totally put off by this whole investigatory debacle? Absolutely. Was I heartbroken again for another disposable black body? Absolutely. But what was the impact of the cry for human connection with white women I once called friends? Friends who I once thought I had some type of connection with because they seemed to have similar values, operate with integrity, have a heart for people, and have an interest in what's right.

The reality is—whether they lack the integrity I once assumed they had or white supremacy is so deeply inbred in their person—they are aloof to the daily compromises of truth and love. But I do know, now more than ever, they are dangerous. And until there is repentance, enlightenment, and redemption, they will never be safe to be called a "friend."

I have many very vivid memories at Baylor, many of which are painfully seared in my mind as "core memories" (to use a reference from the movie *Inside Out*). But this was indeed a core memory for me...

Sallie and I had learned to be comfortable with the very disconnected "supervisory style" of our boss, Driskell. Back then, Sallie and I may have processed it in real-time in various ways—but Driskell managed a lot of different departments and was much more concerned with the more high-risk areas for the institution (i.e., the Department of Public Safety). She was inherently a poor supervisor who wasn't overly concerned with the Equity Office, didn't quite understand the nuances of the work we did, and essentially trusted that whatever we were doing, as long as it wasn't breaking something, was fine.

We also could have been so removed from her office space across the highway that it was very much out of sight, out of mind. Either way, we had settled into the autonomy of managing ourselves.

We kept track of our days off and turned them in to her when we met bi-weekly, and we updated her on whatever projects or cases were on our docket in those same meetings. Now, as we all know, once you are removed from the haze of a trauma-infused situation that you've aggressively coped with, never denying yourself of the hope of something greater for you, your department, and the university, you can see much more clearly. What's crystal clear to me now, and was not too long removed from the madness, was that the Equity Office was indeed a joke.

We had no real power, no real authority, or any real impact (as best as they could control). This is why her management over us was miniscule. She knew that we were two little black girls who were being puppeteered to make the university look like they were actually doing something, as it related to equity. If anybody challenged whether Baylor had their appropriate pieces in place, they could pull out Brittney and Sallie to showboat.

They, of course, wouldn't let us do too much speaking but kept us close enough to check a box. Yet, she and I *always* remained hopeful. Bringing new ideas, new proposals, creative solutions that were tabled, shelved, or squelched in their tracks. Many, if not all, of which were brought out after I resigned and George Floyd had been murdered.

Nevertheless, back to my vivid memory. Sallie was a widowed mother of three who often had to leave the office to tend to children as needed. She enjoyed and appreciated the flexibility of our minuscule management because it allowed her to care for her family well. At the beginning of my tenure in HR and the Equity Office, Sallie was my supervisor. I remember obsessively checking in with her about when I was going to lunch, when I was coming back, when I was leaving, and if I came in late.

Sallie, having worked for the university for decades, constantly insisted, "We are all grown here, hun. Just get your work done and go do what you gotta do."

This was a refreshing new perspective, given the very brief but traumatic run I had with my first supervisor at Baylor. More on her later, but let's say she laid a *strong* foundation of trauma for me. Sallie helped me heal and relax. I was and had always been a woman of really strong and intense integrity. One of the scariest things to me was doing anything that put me in a position to question my integrity, which brings me back to the seared memory.

It was a Wednesday or Thursday. This was right around the time that we were drafting evaluations in preparation for a meeting with our supervisors. This would have also been about two months after I was denied—for the third time—to be a candidate for consideration as the AVP of Equity. They had recently hired someone we'll call "Carson" and Laura Johnson as the assistant and associate VPs.

I had shared with both of them (separately) that I had applied for the position myself. The goal of my communication with them was so that they would not be tainted in any way by anyone about my position and commitment to serve under them. I wanted to be honest and forthright and clear about my heart and intentions to support our equity efforts as the team that we were.

Sallie and I's relationship with Carson was very close. We were like a tight little family. We talked about everything, encouraged each other on all fronts, and kept one another's secrets sacred. I had a healthy working relationship with Laura prior to her applying for the position of AVP, and despite my feelings about her lack of qualifications and deceptive practices that landed her in the position, I was committed to continuing our good working relationship.

I thought the best way to do that was to have a very honest conversation with her but ease any fear she might have that I want to see her fail or that I would undermine her efforts in any way. Once we talked, she seemed to be very empathetic of my journey and position—she even apologized for what I had been through, unbeknownst to her. I left her office very much at peace with our conversation and still hoping for the best.

So, this mid-week work day was really not unusual in any way. My mom was visiting as she did every three to four months around one of the kids' birthdays. It was a beautiful day outside, and at least one time during her visits, there was an unspoken obligation to take her to Magnolia. The frequency with which she expected and enjoyed her Magnolia runs never ceased to amaze me, yet never surprised me.

That day was a particularly warm February day, so we decided I would forgo my lunch hour and leave the office a couple of hours early. Per our norm, I communicated with Sallie that I'd be headed out, as we often did with one another, set my out-of-office (OOO) email in the event someone emailed me and wanted an immediate response, and headed out the door mid-to-late afternoon.

We had a lovely afternoon at Magnolia—we very much enjoyed our time together as a family. That particular day, I do recall going back up to my office around 5 or 6 PM because there were a few things I wanted to finish up. I had not been in the office long before I noticed that I had received an email from Driskell shortly after leaving that day. It had appeared that she had emailed Sallie and I about a matter and received my OOO email.

Upon receiving that email, she *very quickly* drafted her usual second-grade level email with improper sentence structures, lack of punctuation, and run-on sentences to say, very explicitly to me, "You didn't OK with me being out of the office. This is unacceptable and inappropriate... in the future, you need to let me know ahead of time so that I can approve your absence..."

Seared. One, because of the pure rage I felt when reading this. At this point in my Baylor tenure, while damaged goods, I was getting more hip to the tactics used to build a case against an employee who had become a little too outspoken, a little too disruptive, or a little less controllable. The writing was on the wall. This isn't only because I had applied three times for a position I was clearly qualified for without any reason as to why I hadn't made it to the first round... ever. But also because I was moving too fluidly and too confidently throughout the university, building relationships and alliances in every direction.

It had clearly become too threatening on a lot of levels. *And* it was eval time. My evaluations to date had been stellar. If she had any hope of supporting demoting or terminating me—or justifying her decisions not to promote me—she had to build her case. And this is where she was starting. But, unfortunately for her, I was not letting that email stand on its own.

I wasted no time responding explicitly to her accusation that I was doing anything outside the practice of what our interactions had been to date. I wanted that documented. Not only did I document it, but I needed additional eyes on the exchange. I made the very intentional and calculated decision to get the higher-powers-that-be's eyes on this mess ASAP. To be honest, I can't remember if I carbon-copied the VP of HR, blind-copied, or forwarded the communication to her. Either way, she was about to know what was going down from the jump.

After responding to Driskell and getting the communication to the VP of HR, I marched right over to the VPs office on the other side of the building to communicate with her directly about how appalled I was regarding this exchange. I was cutting off this "build a case" at the knees. You want to send this black woman into fight mode? Accuse her of operating with a lack of integrity if you want to, but she *will* be seeing red.

This exchange with the VP, whom I would have considered a "friend" or "mentor" or even "ally," was game-changing. As I stood in her office and asked for her perspective on this situation and how I should respond, she minimized it, as she always had, but in such a jolly, playful, and happy-go-lucky manner, it was easy to get lost in the sauce of her dismissiveness. She made a lot of flippant comments in our interaction, but the glaring statement she made, unprompted by me or my perspective, was "It's not like she's trying to build a case against you or anything."

Immediately, I was frozen where I stood. How did she know that's what I was thinking? Unless that was a typical play in the book. I hadn't mentioned that or alluded to "building a case against me." In that moment, I had simply wanted to get her perspective—as my mentor—on how to respond and move forward with a supervisor questioning my integrity. The VP cleared it up in that moment—she was indeed building a case against me. And you, my supposed ally, refuse to validate the possibility of what is happening. You know why—*doot doot doot Robyn Driskell doot doot doot*—the confirmations kept rolling in as the VPs phone began to ring, loudly broadcasting to both of us that her friend and sorority sister, Driskell, was calling.

They were in one another's pockets and always would be. I was foolish to think that this white woman in power would ever align with this little black girl. The bond and alliance they had with one another squelched any call, conviction, or empathy she ever had or would ever have for me. I didn't need to hear or see anymore. If I had any questions in my mind before those moments, they dissipated into a puff of reality—I was beginning to realize that I was on my own.

***

My last and final cry for help to a white "friend" in power happened shortly after COVID-19 hit the fan—early April 2020.

For most of us, early 2020 was an absolute whirlwind. As I sit here and reflect on those first six months, they were the most pivotal and traumatic moments in my 33 years of life. I guess you can say that my "Jesus year" launched me into a deeper and richer calling than I ever could have known was on the horizon for me or the Wardlaws. But the process of that crossover was painful. I would be lying if I said it wasn't. As God has constantly reminded me on this faith journey: Even in the fire, He is there. But that doesn't mean the fire ain't hot.

It's very clear to me now—and was relatively clear to me then—that I was desperately fighting depression and anxiety at a level I hadn't seen. The thing that made it that much harder is that I'm a "power through" type of person. If I don't stop and acknowledge or reflect on what's happening, I don't have to be bogged down with owning it and not knowing what to do with it.

I think anxiety has always been in the backdrop of my life, but my body holds it tightly in my gut. It's not until I'm randomly throwing up or I'm in urgent care because of excruciating pain in my abdomen that I say, *Oops, I think my body has been keeping score of what I'm ignoring.*[5]

As I mentioned, that year was hard for all of us for many reasons. But for me, thankfully, the innermost intimate circle of my life was minimally affected by COVID. I recognize that life looked a lot different for others outside of my home on Windsor Avenue in Waco. But coming into 2020, I was looking to re-establish and accept in a real way that all the sacrifices my family had made by uprooting our lives in Virginia, leaving everything we knew—including our families, our home, our professional success, our familiarity, our financial stability—to follow a call that we believed the Lord was going to manifest seeds of faith in a real way, was just not coming to fruition the way we imagined.

Gary's part-time practice was a great outlet and follow-through on what we believed the Lord opened up for him to do, but it in no way was sustaining us. Yes, I was still on my near six-figure salary, but with little to no real responsibilities, no direct reports, four promotion denials at this point, and a career at Baylor that was stagnant at best—or on a trajectory for a constructive termination[11] at worst.

Things were hard. But, as usual, Gary and I maintained our optimistic posture, believing that our steps of faith were absolutely not in vain, we did not hear wrong, and my willingness to take a demotion to come out here would manifest fruit soon. In January 2020, after an interview process for the Assistant Vice President of Equity, for which I mentioned I was not given an initial interview, the university decided to hire Carson—a Black man with a master's degree and comparable years of experience as myself.

While disappointed with the disregard for my commitment to Baylor, the career investment in both the Title IX and Diversity, Equity, Inclusion (DEI)/Civil Rights spaces and my successful projects and relationships across the university, I was still pleased and relieved to see them put a Black man in this elevated leadership position.

However, that relief was short-lived. Not only did Baylor decide to put him in this position with his two direct reports in the Equity Office, but they had simultaneously decided to put an inexperienced white woman as his supervisor. But let's be frank, shall we—it was to make sure these niggers in the Equity Office didn't get too far out of line.

This was a lot to take in. But, the usual power through posture got in position, as did the strong, intentional, and authentic posture of integrity. After these announcements were made, I made it a point to have a very candid, honest, but loving conversation with *both* of them. I needed both of my new supervisors to know that I was there to support the team and the work of our call. As I stated, I was honest about my disappointment and what I was working through, but I needed them to hear from me that I was in their corner—in spite of any narrative that Driskell would try to spin about me.

Carson and I always had a very transparent, healthy, and supportive working relationship. Laura and I had at one point, too. But as the months rolled on, it became obvious that, in spite of my transparency and commitment to bring my full self to work, the narrative was being spun. In spite of Laura having spent time in my home, celebrating our housewarming, planning playdates, and her previous consistent positive comments about Sallie and I's competence in DEI/Civil Rights, something was shifting—and shifting quickly.

February was evaluation prep time. I was in an odd spot. Driskell would likely be the one completing my eval as she had been my supervisor all of

2019 and was just transitioning to now having several people between her and I, which was the way she liked it. She would no longer have to deal directly with my questions she couldn't answer, subject matter conversations that were over her head, or navigating the constant barrage of accolades about the work I was doing with her peers.

We were all expected to complete our evaluations around February and meet with our supervisors to discuss those evaluations in early March. Unsurprisingly, Driskell rescheduled our meeting several times. Could her schedule have been prohibiting her from doing so? Perhaps. But the more glaring reason was for the sheer fact that she was going to have to look me in the eye and, with a straight face, explain the plummet in my evaluation.

What had so drastically changed in my performance that you could speak about with a clear conscience to justify an average of 3.9 (Mastery) to barely a 3 (Competence)? She needed *something* to support these promotional denials and the other surprises she had for me on the horizon.

So, as fate would have it, COVID hit before she and I got a chance to meet. Weeks went by, and everyone was working from home. I found out that not only were she and I not going to be meeting to discuss my evaluation, but she had already uploaded it into the HR system. Without a review, without my signature. She had documented this blasphemous evaluation with no consequences or accountability for doing so.

So what did I do? You already know. I reached out to my white friend in high places, the VP of HR. "Cheryl, please help me understand this. Is this protocol? How do I refute something like this? Please help me navigate this as soon as possible."

Her reply was brief but unbelievably telling. "Hi Brittney, I think you should try to work this out with Robyn before I insert myself..."

The writing was on the wall. They had officially taken position to feed me to the wolves. And there was nothing I could do about it. At that time, reality really started to set in. There were no lifelines anymore. I had been in HR far too long not to recognize the signs. They were getting in position to get rid of me. If they couldn't build a case for my termination, they were going to make things so incredibly difficult that my termination would be constructive. And COVID was just what they needed to assist in the latter.

As universities and businesses scrambled all over the country to make sense of what to do with their business practices and employees, Baylor was doing the same. In that process, they created a "program" where they were "reallocating" employees who had jobs that "required on-campus presence" and placed them in another area that needed assistance or was looking to hire. But they were now in a hiring freeze. So the alleged thought was, well, there are people that "aren't doing anything," so we'll use them in the meantime. The story I was given was that they would put me in a "comparable level position."

My colleague and I were told very early in the game that we would likely be a part of this program because there were no on-campus opportunities available, and we didn't have much we were doing (especially being in the Equity, Civil Rights, and DEI space as Asian students and faculty all over campus were being actively bullied as the "China virus" changed everyone's lives).[6] But nevertheless, ironically, we were going to be put into the pool. At this time, we had zero context of how frequently this was happening nor how many employees were in the pool, but what became obvious very quickly was that we were the first ones in it.

To this day, the strategic and manipulative layers that were at play to dismantle the Equity Office are astounding. Simultaneously, our new supervisor, Carson, was on his way to a PIP (Performance Improvement Plan). Month three of being hired. As a very tight and close-knit team, we talked daily. He was communicating with us regularly that he had every intention of staying and doing everything he could to see the vision of what we wanted to do in the Equity Office come to fruition. However, within days of having had these conversations, he was communicating to us that he would be leaving and couldn't discuss it any further.

But he didn't need to. I had been where he was three very long years prior. He needed to say no more. My colleague had been in HR for over 20 years, and I had not only seen some years, but sat on the side of the table he now found himself on. Say no more, brotha—say no more.

As this unfolded, my colleague and I were quickly pitted against one another. In spite of supervisory threats not to communicate with one another, our friendship and sisterhood ran much deeper than their threats. We confided in one another, prayed for one another, and cried for one another as they made it clear that she would now *be* the Equity Office reporting to Laura, and I was on my way out.

I would be assuming an entry level position at the Texas Hunger Initiative, responding to emails of parents looking for meal boxes that had not arrived at their homes, and reporting to a student worker. In an effort to humbly offer her brokenness and transparency with me, she sobbed, "I know I'm a 'yes' man, and that's why they're keeping me…"

I don't think it could get any more demoralizing than this. My ten years of experience in higher education, my doctorate degree, and my strong performance evaluations couldn't save me. At this point, I was a competent, confident, Black woman who had officially made too many white women insecure to sustain any professional growth at this institution. With no other lifelines, I began to get my ducks in order to have representation and prepare for my departure.

As matter of fact as my moves were, my body kept the score. In those six months, not only did I find myself at Urgent Care with gastritis, but I had lost ten to fifteen pounds and suffered a miscarriage. And as much as

I wanted to feel like I was managing and weathering this storm, my body was clearly telling me otherwise.

Chapter 3: Pet to Threat

Our transition to Waco, Texas, was sudden and unexpected. In the Fall of 2016, Gary and I were at the top of our game in every way. I was successfully running my own office as an executive director at the age of 30; we were homeowners in a beautiful suburban development just outside Lynchburg; Gary was getting great experience under some powerful mentors at the local hospital and even worked part-time at a private practice being mentored by the practice owner. All of this while he was in a doctoral program at a decently prestigious institution.

We had a beautiful, black circle of friends and lived within a fifteen to twenty-five-minute drive of our brother, sister, and nephews. We were intricately involved in our local church, and our marriage was good. I guess you could say we felt that we were winning at life, and it felt like the only place to go from there was up. Life was good. So to say our move was sudden and unexpected is an understatement.

When we got to Waco, there were many who were close to us that had a lot of questions and concerns about this move. We had moments of wondering because of the challenges that came early on. However, God was so kind and faithful to give us tiny—but very real—confirmations along the way. I have some very vivid memories of those small but affirming moments.

Our first few weeks there, we went to every single basketball game we could. We loved the energy of the stadium and the legitimacy of being at a Big 12 school! On one occasion, I remember us standing in line to get our tickets and a middle-aged white man striking up a conversation with us while we were waiting for the ticket booth to open up. After he asked a few conversational questions, he quickly discovered that I was the newest part of the infamous Title IX Office.

I can't lie, the position came with a lot of respect and "reverence." I now understand—at an even deeper level—why there was such reverence for someone who was hailed for saving their precious Baylor from the spotlight and humiliation of sexual violence scandals.

I don't remember too many more details about our conversation after that. I just remember his attentiveness to our conversation. The next day, I left the office with Kristan to go to some type of meeting around the lunch hour. While we were out, she was very intentional about "introducing" her new shiny deputy coordinator to everyone we came into contact with. But, the thing was, there were several introductions there was no need for because we were already well acquainted. I can't say that I noticed right away that she was bothered—until we got back to the office.

When we got back that day, her administrative assistant greeted us at the door with her messages. She proceeded to share that a professor had called to speak with someone about a situation. Before Kristan could complete her sentence to say she'd give them a callback, her admin interrupted and sheepishly said, "Actually, he specifically wants to speak to Brittney..."

Then, she shot a look at me and spitefully said, "Why does he want to speak to you?" I was embarrassed and didn't have a real answer at the moment. But, essentially, people were connecting with us in every direction. It was affirming that we were right where we were supposed to be. But it was also the beginning of the unraveling of Kristan, her insecurities, and the process of putting this "pet" down.

How do I know? Because these instances continued. There was an assistant VP in Student Life that we'll call Mary, who adored me and our family. She was a 70-something-year-old white lady who had worked at Baylor for forty or fifty years and literally knew everyone. She went out of her way to make meaningful connections between humans, and she did not hold back for us.

I left for maternity leave at the end of February. Shortly after returning from maternity leave in mid-April—after much of the soder and salt had been laid for the venom of insecurity to begin to choke Kristan out—Mary called the Title IX Office. I learned early on that Kristan was infamous for disappearing from the office. No one really knew what or where she was, but she was "very busy," so we didn't ask many questions. Nevertheless, Mary was in the process of coordinating a very public signing of a Memorandum of Understanding (MOU)[7] with the university and the local advocacy center. She had tried to no avail to get a hold of Kristan and had made multiple attempts to request her presence at this event.

She eventually reached out to me and thought it would be more than appropriate to request my presence at the event. Of course, I was honored and excited about the opportunity to be included in this very important event for the campus and the greater Waco community. However, I vividly remember being scolded by Kristan when I reached out to her about attending. She belittled and shamed me for thinking it appropriate to ask because that was not my place, and there were other things I "should be more concerned about."

She said things like, "Maybe you should be more concerned about the list of tasks I asked you to complete days ago that you still have yet to get to me." She then proceeded to have her administrative assistant attend the event, sign on behalf of the Title IX Office, and be published in the university and local papers. That same loyal administrative assistant a short time later disclosed to me that the task of things Kristan had delegated for me to complete within a few short days, two of them she had been trying to finish for months.

In real-time, I was perplexed. In hindsight, it's clear as day. This type of attention, notoriety, and connection to influential individuals was way too threatening. The much safer decision for the sake of her ego was to send an hourly employee straight out of college to represent the office.

***

I'm not sure about the immediate impact this next situation had on Kristan and her feeling threatened, but I do know it significantly bolstered the respect, appeal, and reputation traction I was quickly gaining all over campus. Early on, she had me attend a meeting with the Counseling Office with her. I do not recall the focus of the meeting, but I do remember how appalled I was with how she interacted with people at this meeting.

The chairs were set up in a square. Everyone had a seat on the outside of the square so that every face was in view. This made it very easy for me to do my best to get a pulse on the vibe. I could see every single face, every single shift, and every twitch of body language. Being new to the university and working really hard to get a read on the environment, this was a perfect opportunity to "see how people worked and ticked," including my new supervisor. Well, needless to say, I sat in controlled and tempered disbelief for much of the meeting.

I knew Kristan and I were the focus of the meeting because Title IX still had everyone's heart and mind at attention. But, I was dumbfounded by how she moved and interacted with the tone of the room. It seemed clear to *me* that these people were not in opposition to the work of our office. However, when people would speak, her responses were abrasive, dismissive, and belittling. I was cringing.

I was doing a lot of calculating in my head and tried to be very discerning about how or when I interjected. Since everyone was facing inward, I could see every eye, read every face, notice every shift, and absorb all the tension that continued to intensify with Kristan's aggressive responses.

There was one moment when I did have an opportunity to tactfully follow up after Kristan made a comment to explain something that exacerbated that aforementioned tension. With all of the wisdom and grace that I could, I spoke up to clarify, de-escalate, and affirm my supervisor as best I could—and the room shifted. I wish I could remember the specifics of what we were discussing. But I do know the conversation was problem-solving focused around the Baylor Title IX recommendations from the Philadelphia firm they hired to help clean up their mess. Nonetheless, whatever it was, I had chosen the right opportunity wisely.

The atmosphere shifted. Tensions were eased. The faces in the room gleamed at me with a pleasant look of disbelief and hope. And in that moment, I was again affirmed. "You're right where you need to be."

After that meeting, my reputation in both the Counseling Center and the Student Life division proceeded me. I was humbled and grateful. But it also fed the venom of the snake preparing to eat me alive. The transition with Kristan was real and it was swift.

You are no longer my shiny pet but a very real threat that must be eaten alive. And that was what she proceeded to do at every opportunity for the six weeks I spent in that office before I was relocated from Title IX to HR.

***

One of the uncanny ways I was able to remain hopeful about the opportunities I believed were waiting for me and an upward career trajectory at Baylor—in spite of being ignored and placated about potential promotions—was the company I kept. As I may mention more than once, my "friends" were Deans, AVPs, Provosts, General Counsel, and Chief Compliance Officers. I guess you could say some of my closest friends—who weren't Black—were in high places.

We dined together, we did life together, we worked on projects together, we drank coffee together. They were also constantly in private meeting rooms with Driskell. Oftentimes, their curiosity and confusion overrode their "decorum." They didn't understand why I wasn't in a different position—a more senior-level position over equity-related matters. Mainly because they were constantly consulting with me about how to navigate various issues in their respective divisions.

I would politely but confidently share with them that I wasn't sure, but I knew in due time, I would be able to operate in the fullness of what I was passionate about and called to do. They disbelievingly shook their heads and let me know they were "going to say something to Robyn." I never encouraged them not to—I welcomed it because, surely, her hearing from these respectable professionals would encourage and affirm to her that I was ready and called to do right by the university in an equity leadership role.

But, of course, these interactions had quite the opposite impact. These "friends" would later come back to me, bewildered at her responses—or lack thereof. "I just don't get it," they'd comment. I'd hear things like, "She changed the subject" or "She acted like she didn't hear me."

I met with her weekly. Not one time did she believe it was important or remotely a priority to mention there were individuals—important individuals—inquiring, encouraging, or affirming my performance and who were supportive of a promotion or recognition. I now understand that there was nothing in her that wanted to see me succeed. I didn't understand the threatening professional that I was.

It took an AVP that I met with regularly for coffee—and who was one of her direct reports—to tell me, "Britt, you're a threat to her. Her insecurities will never allow her to promote, highlight, encourage, or support you in what you do."

I often thought he was gassing me. I know this has been a place of personal growth because previously, I always struggled to believe or accept the positive statements individuals like him would say about me. Perhaps this was how my imposter syndrome[8] would show up. Nonetheless, the only reference she ever made in regards to someone (specifically a provost) talking to her about me was to express her irritation. Allow me to expound.

I was hosting a book club with eight to ten hand-chosen influential leaders I believed to be in a position of great influence for racial equity at the institution. I thought these individuals just needed a little bit of encouragement or support to be able to do so in their respective areas—enter book club. There was a provost who I didn't know very well, but was encouraged by a provost I was friends with to invite him. This awkward white man ended up being a fully engaged and enthusiastic participant. I was thrilled to have him, and we quickly formed a very fun bond.

He was not shy about that bond. With anyone. Even if it meant he was going to yell across the parking lot to speak to me or go out of his way to communicate his excitement on a weekly—or even daily—basis about how much he loved me and my book club. So, in one of our weekly meetings with Driskell, she mentioned in passing, with much irritation, an interaction she had with this provost about the book club. The only thing I remember her sharing specifically was her response to him, which was, "Calm down, it's not that serious," followed by a roll of her eyes.

But none of it mattered. As much as I hoped that these interactions, recommendations, and inquiries would help support a case for my promotion, all it did was remind Driskell of the threat that I was to her. Unbeknownst to me, the more those interactions happened, my chances of promotion were dwindling, and my threatening presence was increasing—setting me up quite nicely for some type of constructive termination down the road.

***

It was early July 2019—my favorite part of the summer—and I was amped up and ready to enjoy this Kirk Franklin concert with Bae and our backstage passes. Our babies were with friends, and we were excited about relishing in a very fun, child-free evening. It was a warm Texas day, and the summer streets were bustling with excitement. We got there nice and early and made our way to the Will Call ticket booth. We were like two kids acting like we were at our first concert, but we felt like two kids who had just gotten the first pick on the playground when they handed us our VIP badges.

We went inside and quickly found our seats, waiting for the opening act to begin. As we sat there, grinning at each other like we were on a first date, taking in the lights and excitement and people filing in, I received a text—8:54 PM. It was from Driskell.

"Did you share the HEED award application with anyone?"

The anxiety I felt at that moment was indescribable yet familiar. With all of the excitement and joy and peace that surrounded me, it suddenly felt as if someone sucked the oxygen out of my body. There were so many things to process at that moment. But in order to give the full context about that moment, we have to rewind to April 2019.

Driskell was generally uninterested in educational matters focused on DEI and race equity, so I always had the pleasure of participating in opportunities that came downstream that she otherwise would have dismissed. Many of those opportunities were life-altering for me, with one being the *Race Equity Institute* sponsored by the Waco Foundation. This was by a special invitation only to the most influential leaders in the city.

As Chief of Staff at BU, Driskell was invited to attend on multiple occasions. Not finding it of priority—or interest, let's be honest—I had the opportunity to attend as her representative. Another such occasion was the Big 12 Chief Diversity Officer (CDO) Conference in 2018 at the University of Oklahoma. I was so giddy to be amongst the ranks of some of the most brilliant and powerful individuals in the Big 12. I was going to soak up every second, every conversation, and every meeting.

I made some amazing connections in that very short weekend. It was another reminder that I *belong* in these ranks. There's no need to be intimidated. God's favor to walk among kings and queens was always being affirmed for me—even when I didn't see it myself. That takes us to April 2019, when Baylor was slated to host the conference. It was another great weekend, but it was also very affirming as I reconnected with those giants I had connected with the previous year.

The hosting process went very well. One of the provosts at the time was the primary host, and she did an amazing job with everyone's support. As the conference wrapped up that weekend, it ended with one final meeting. I couldn't tell you many details of what was discussed in that meeting, with the exception of one topic—the HEED (Higher Education Excellence in Diversity) Award.

Now, my good friend, David, who has since retired, was the CDO at West Virginia University and had been for many years. He was also the chair of that conference. He asked all of the CDOs whose institutions had been awarded the HEED Award to raise their hands. Most of the room raised their hands, and he encouraged the one to two institutions in the room that had not (Baylor being one) to apply because he believed it was within reach for anyone.

At that moment, I remember Driskell motioning to one of her assistants to make note of that, and within a few short weeks, many of us all over campus were feverishly gathering information and filling in the application on a shared document. I remember it being fast and furious. But I also remember taking some vacation time sometime that June.

By the time I got back after Sallie and I provided our contribution, there was little to no time for me to review the application. Everyone who contributed was told something to the effect of "review and let us know if you have any feedback, updates, or questions." So, when I returned from vacation, I thought the application had been submitted. Prior to taking my time off, in the process of providing our updates from the "Equity Office," I was vexed about the whole thing. Baylor was a sham when it came to diversity, and I couldn't believe we were going to apply to be rewarded for our efforts. It felt dishonest and downright embarrassing.

I had confided in David about what I should do. As a believer, a seasoned professional, and a friend (not at Baylor), I felt like he was the best person to talk to. He was very wise and encouraging in our conversation. With that, I uploaded our office information into the application. When I returned, I messaged Driskell that I had some questions for her. She let me know that it was too late and the application had been submitted. She asked if my concerns were urgent, to which I replied that they weren't. And that was that.

So, when I received that text a couple of weeks later, the oxygen left my body for two very clear reasons. The first was utter panic that my having confided in David had somehow gotten back to her, and that was in some way interpreted as betraying the institution. The second reason was the distrust that she had for me was communicated in a very accusatory text message—an outright attack on my integrity, my most sacred asset.

As 2019 marched on, even as I continued to blow on my little flame of hope whenever possible, the reasons Driskell would never promote me continued to pile up and cement—making significant strides at snuffing out any hope I continued to carry.

***

In the initial stages of the negotiations or communication that I would be leaving, I met with the General Counsel and Associate Counsel, who I, at the time, considered one of my dearest friends. During this meeting, she even cried, communicating their desire to work something out and for me to stay at Baylor. They wanted to make changes and felt I could help make those changes. While I communicated that that would not be an option, she attempted to respond but was unable to do so because she was fighting her tears...

As the negotiation process went on, I was sent a version of the severance agreement. As I was sweeping and cleaning my house one day, listening to music, the song *Strong God* by Kirk Franklin came on. A song about a hard-fought fight against injustices based on the color of our skin. I was reminded of how my ancestors have been fighting this fight for centuries. I wondered if they ever felt like we were always on the losing side. Then, the Spirit reminded me that He's always fighting for us. There is more happening than we can see. I shouldn't grow weary in what I can see in the natural realm.

What I saw in the natural world were the clauses in a severance agreement. A severance agreement for someone who was tokenized for years at Baylor University. I was a young, spirited, motivated, attractive African American female with a beautiful family who truly made the university look good. Whether I was representing them on community panels, as a spokesperson for charitable organizations, or asked by constituents all over campus to be a part of their projects or initiatives—it was clear there was a strong season of "pet." But, it's incredible how a simple clause in a severance agreement communicates how vanishing that status is as a Black female who was beginning to truly understand and be proud of her blackness.

The clause read, "Ms. Wardlaw agrees that she will not seek or apply for work at Baylor. If offered work at Baylor, Ms. Wardlaw agrees not to accept such work." And just like that—an ousted threat. As I reflected on this clause, I wanted to vomit. A wave of feelings and emotions hit me, from nausea to rage. The fight of our ancestors whirled around me—imagining what it must have felt like not to see any progress during their lifetime. Yet still, they fought the fight of oppression and went to their unmarked graves, trusting the Lord and trusting that the fight would never be in vain.

Today, we fight the same fight but in a different way. The fight for many of us is one of the mind and heart. As we see our brothers' and sisters' bodies warred upon daily, we feel psychologically murdered in the streets. And then we go to work in our corporate positions and expect to believe the nation has come such a long way because of where we are professionally. We're reminded that we're not viewed as any more valuable than our Black brothers and sisters gunned down in the street when we're discarded professionally after showing too much of our blackness in these white spaces. Once your "black" is out, so are you. Just like that. Like an old toy that no longer has value. An old toy that's been played with and used for its purposes and suddenly loses its value.

As I read and learn and study more and more about white supremacy, I'm appalled by my twenty-five to thirty years of willingly being this shiny new toy, used and discarded. I thought I was "helping our people" by playing the part that made white people comfortable and furthered their agendas because I thought they'd ultimately give me a seat at their table. I begged for that seat. I slaved for that seat. Only to be told over and over again that I wasn't ready for that seat. That seat would come soon. I needed to stop begging for my dignity. I needed to stop begging for a seat at the table and build my own damn table.

Build a table, people. We have the skills, the talents, the drive, the anointing. Build a table.

Chapter 4: Pushed Out, Burnt Out, or Sell Out

What does being pushed out look like? A formal reference to a pushout is very much like the legal definition of "constructive termination" or "constructive discharge." This is when an employee's resignation or retirement may be found not to be voluntary because the employer has created a hostile or intolerable work environment or the employer has applied other forms of pressure or coercion that forced the employee to quit or resign.

Well, that's definitely my story.

How does burnout appear? According to the World Health Organization, burnout is a syndrome conceptualized as resulting from chronic workplace stress... characterized by three dimensions: feelings of energy depletion or exhaustion, increased mental distance from one's job, or feelings of negativism or cynicism related to one's job. I've got a few stories to share there as well.

And lastly, the sellout. An online Merriam-Webster dictionary definition yields "to betray one's cause or associates, especially for personal gain." A much more sensitive area to identify and share when it comes specifically to the Black culture because of the intra-cultural complexities of the difficult choices we are making to survive or attempt to thrive in a white supremacist paradigm. Unfortunately, I have stories identified here as well.

***

Listening to Dr. Jemar Tisby's podcast *Pass the Mic*, I hear him say this phrase: "Pushed out, burnt out, or sell out." It hit on all fronts for me. I start going through my story in my mind, thinking about questions I've asked myself and others. I start reflecting on close black friends that I've worked alongside over the years and how they have entered one of these spaces already or are headed for these spaces quickly. It was enlightening and deeply thought-provoking.

This also speaks to how pivotal Jemar Tisby has been in my anti-racism journey and departure from Baylor University. A few years back—roughly late 2018, early 2019—I heard him say on his *Footprints* podcast, "Stop begging for a seat at their table. Build your own." And it rocked me to my core. It almost made me feel sick.

I had spent years at Baylor University and even at Liberty University, begging for a seat at the table. Knowing and believing that I had something of value to bring to these organizations. I was convinced that hard work and a little time and savvy navigating would land me that well-deserved seat. I was doing my very best to present myself in every light and angle as someone who *was* seen as valuable.

My vocational hopes and dreams were tied up in higher education. I knew the land—specifically white evangelical, southern higher education. I knew the cultures. I had effectively learned to be dynamic and impactful—all while keeping white people comfortable. I learned a lot of this in my rearing as a child in a white evangelical church in South Jersey. There are slight differences.

What I had not fully accounted for was the influence and power of the insecure white women in power, and Baylor was full of them. Granted, there definitely were powerful, secure white women, but the poison and violence—as Rachel Ricketts says so eloquently—of the former is lethal. And while there were secure and powerful white women in my corner, when it was time to stand in the gap for me and potentially risk something on their part, the silence was deafening.

After crossing one too many insecure white women in power by challenging the status quo, presenting new ideas or concepts, building relationships and networks, and making a name for myself in spaces all over campus, they deployed this violence to murder me psychologically, emotionally, mentally, and ultimately, professionally.

***

After I started my tenure in Human Resources after being recruited and then forced out of the Title IX Office, my Black colleague and I were tasked with creating and building out the EEO arm of Human Resources. We were given little to no resources but were given what we thought was great autonomy. I used this space to introduce some of the previous skills and experiences I had in earlier roles in my career. One of those experiences included my training in conflict resolution.

Anyone who has ever worked in compliance or any type of investigative arm of an organization knows that, in the end, no one wins. The best-case scenario depends on who you're asking. After ravaging through to find "the truth" about what happened–usually both respondent and complainant are left to pick up the pieces of their lives in the wake, regardless of the outcome. So, in an effort to be more unifying, healing, and even progressive, I suggested mediation formats for appropriate claims coming to the office. One of the first opportunities to put this into practice came with a situation involving a Black male resident director who had concerns about bullying from his white female residents in the form of reporting his mentor relationship with a black female resident assistant.

He reported his concerns to his superiors—a white female director and a white male assistant director. Ultimately, the situation escalated, culminating in a conflict with the directors and this black male RD. Because of the nature of the situation, my colleague and I made a critically thoughtful recommendation to do mediation with each party. This was an option the RD was open to trying because he trusted us and our advice. He was hopeful for less contentious options to resolve what had become a very stressful situation for him, hindering his ability to do his job well. Our hearts did go out to him. He genuinely wanted to do what was right, needed someone to trust, and wanted to be able to move forward in his role as an RD.

My colleague and I were really hopeful about the potential resolution of the situation. We started the process by speaking with the HRC (human resource consultant) about this particular area. From our early navigation of being in the EEOC[10] position and being housed in HR, she and I thought we were doing right by everyone by communicating with the parties regularly and keeping in touch with the HRC. What we quickly realized in this EEOC role was that we were on an island.

Employee "respondents" saw the HRCs as their personal advocates and the EEOC as their antagonizers. This alignment quickly put us in very contentious positions with both the HRC and their departments. Trust me, we didn't understand this from the outset—our collaborative spirit and naivete walked us right into professional death traps, unarmed. This was one of the most costly situations to learn this paradigm.

So, as I mentioned, we had this brilliant idea to create a mediation situation. We went to Cassidy, who was the HRC, to discuss the likelihood of proceeding with this option and explain what it would entail. We did our best to keep her abreast of our conversations with the RD as well as the various conversations we had with his assistant director and director, who, at the time, we thought we had good working relationships with—particularly with the director, the white female.

But as we got closer to being able to mediate, the assistant director, the white male, began communicating with us less and less. Eventually, we would only hear from him through Cassidy. Then, when Cassidy was communicating with us, her communication became a bit more contentious, accusatory, and a little antagonistic. Eventually Rob, the assistant director, agreed to have a meeting with this young RD, but he requested that my colleague and I not be allowed to be in attendance.

What sense did that make? Why would we coordinate a mediation, send this 20-something-year-old Black man into a room with a middle-aged white male supervisor, his middle-aged white woman supervisor, and their close-to-middle-age white HR representative, *without* myself or my colleague—the two black females who were coordinating a conversation for everyone's voices to be appropriately heard?

Of course, in real-time, my colleague and I did not understand how we got here or why we would agree to this demand or "request," so we arranged a meeting with the HRC and her supervisor to talk through the situation and alternative resolution approaches in case they needed some clarity on the goals.

Well, it quickly became apparent that this contentious and territorial posture of Rob was not in isolation. This HRC was living in that camp as well. In attempting to have an amenable conversation about the mediation option, she was defensive, aggressive, and postured in defensiveness for much of the meeting. How did we know? Her dialogue, glare, and red face gave her away. It created several awkward moments because her level of intensity did not match the energy of the reason for the meeting, which was to understand the goals of mediation and take steps to set everyone up for success.

I do not remember many details of the conversation at that meeting. I just remember the aggressive advocacy of the HRC and "her parties." I also remember the realization that HR was not our ally, and while it would have been nice, we were not all aligned with the same goals. Our goal was to do what was right by human beings by any means necessary. HR's goal was to protect the university. Protecting the university meant protecting its leadership and stakeholders.

People like this young black male were casualties and potential pain points for the university that needed to be dealt with and quickly disposed of. So, for the white male assistant director to request my colleague and me not to be there made perfect sense. We would be leveling the playing field for this young man. And the reality was, in this system, the playing field was never meant to be leveled. It was not the way the game was played—leveling meant putting white stakeholders at a major disadvantage, and those were not the rules of engagement.

So, with that, no matter how much my colleague and I thought we were doing right by people and the university, we were causing a disruption in a system that was running exactly the way it was intended to and making lots of enemies along the way.

And what ended up happening? HR thought it best that we not try to continue with the mediation. They decided they would just have a talk with the young black man. But shortly before that, some "concerning messages" were brought to our attention in regard to a group conversation he had with his team. These "messages" were about him quoting an "inappropriate song" as a joke, which was "very concerning to them and his professionalism."

So, just like that, in alignment with HR's normal playbook, his professionalism was now under review. The mediation was off. And they would be meeting with him to address the professionalism concerns. Within a few short weeks, it was brought to their attention that an "important protocol" response with one of his residents a few months back was missed. And within a month, this man was terminated.

***

I find it interesting that, of the countless black professionals I knew at Baylor while I was there, so many have since left. I do recognize that a whole pandemic happened, and people's lives changed. But, I also recognized a pretty significant difference in the longevity of black people at Baylor. For me, it begs the question of why we don't have the type of longevity that our white counterparts have. Do we want to? Absolutely. It's a great setup. Master pays well, our families have stability, and the school has notoriety. However, many, if not all, have sadly fallen into one of those categories—push out, burn out, sell out—*or* are on a very clear trajectory to do so in the near future.

The "push out" came with range. Myself and my Soror[12] who "retired" from Baylor as an OG for representing a voice of DEI all over campus, were two of the classic examples of "push out." From what I am able to gather (because, like most, she is unable to discuss the details of her "retirement"), she left with all the bells and whistles, with her signature on the dotted line, and some extra money in her savings. And then you have me, taking steps toward negotiating with $125,000 on the table and an obligation to be sworn to secrecy about all I've seen and experienced indefinitely.

Recognizing that we both were higher-level staff members who could be significantly more damaging to Baylor and its image if we spoke out.

But the other end of the spectrum yielded people like this young black male RD, who was terminated with two weeks of pay and little to no time to gather his things. As well as an entry-level program coordinator at the School of Nursing who had the audacity to make accusations against the dean and her assistant dean, only to be left with a dead-end EEO claim, anxiety, and medical issues, as well as termination on the end of a medical leave because of the mental anguish she had faced.

The "burnout" is sneaky and brutal. I saw that one manifest in my closest circles. This was mid-level managers who were so close to the ones in charge that they were typically the ones doing all of the work and watching their supervisors get the credit. They were OK with it, though, because there was a hope, a sense, or even a perception that all of this hard work would not be in vain. At the right time, they would be elevated to their rightful positions because their game-changing contributions were undeniable, right? Wrong.

Of the primary three individuals for which I watched this ring true, I watched two of the three (five-year tenure and fifteen-year tenure) begin to settle into deep resentment as the reality of their circumstances simmered—only for their fires to be brought to life again through the process of being wooed and pursued by another organization. The reminders of their value ignited the fire once again, and all three eventually accepted these new positions at the upper-level management role that they always knew they were capable of.

And the "sell out" is no less deadly to the perpetuation of a system that sneaks to devour. Two of the most potent examples of this outcome bring two individuals to my mind. One is very sensitive and painful to talk about, admittedly, because of the closeness of our relationship—our sisterhood. She was the classic example of doing what you feel like is your only option for the sake of providing for your family.

Baylor pays well and is overall very kind to their employees in generous ways. However, for the black mind and body, there is a lot of unseen damage done because of how many of us feel like the only true option is to comply with their practices—refusing to speak up, which would inevitably put a target on one's back. She refused to be targeted for the sake of providing, which is, ultimately, for personal gain. More selfless, to say the least, but personal gain nonetheless.

The other potent example is the individual who now represents the voice of POC at the university. He played his hand just right, and the university and its leadership felt very safe with him. The problem is that individuals like him are not often found in the mix with the communities of color. And it begs the question, how do you know how to advocate for the community at large if you are not in tune with the community at large? Playing your hand right and being in a position of influence and power is the priority—not "career-risking" advocacy. More on him later.

Chapter 5: Grief and Loss

I have recently had a lot of daydreams about my relationships at Baylor. I had a lot of people I would have called my friends in high positions. High positions that made a clear choice not to compromise the comforts of power to align with the likes of a branded and ousted token negro. It's hard to think about at times.

All of the lunch dates, the invites to birthday parties and housewarmings, the baby shower gifts, warm embraces with my little girls—it's truly so much to think about. Was it time wasted? Do I feel discarded like that old toy? How much time and energy do I spend remembering these relationships that have long washed up on shore like that tattered shoe in the ocean? I often wonder if they miss me. How easy was it for them to move on, knowing that to stand by or with me was a much higher cost than they were willing to pay?

Some of the people of color I considered friends are still with me—in the shadows. None of them really have significant positions of power that actually would be affected by our associations. Most not anything above a director—given enough power to look like the institution has done something of significance, all the while, until very recently, still only one person of color at the level of a chair.

I always thought it was interesting that, on any given day, I might be going to lunch with a dear friend who was a chair or a provost or a VP or dean. Those were the circles that I ran in with ease. I never felt out of place, I never felt beneath my friends. It was always very natural and fluid. So, it often begged the question, why did all of these people in positions of power feel they had a connection with little old me? An equity officer in the second story of Clifton Robinson Tower who was a "manager" of no one.

As many know, I left Liberty University at the age of 30 as an executive director of a team with four direct reports and twelve to fifteen dotted-line reports. I knew taking a position as the Deputy Title IX Coordinator on paper was a demotion, but I also knew that, in the natural realm, with the success I was having at Liberty, my work ethic, and leadership intuition, it would only be a matter of time before I would have the opportunity to prove myself at Baylor.

When I arrived at Baylor University, I was 34 weeks pregnant. I worked for approximately four weeks before going on maternity leave in a new state, new city, and new school of employment. However, Gary and I did not waste any time getting acclimated to our new city. Fortunately, our daughter Justice was a reasonable newborn, and my recovery was mild, so we were always on the move. We attended sporting games, local venues, and events in the city and made quick connections and relationships in and around the institution. It was like we were neon—everywhere we went, we were glowing, and people were attracted to us. For us, it felt like a warm affirmation that we had heard the Lord correctly and were right where we were supposed to be.

My four weeks in the office before going on leave were... slow. It was as if my first supervisor, Kristan—also my former law school colleague who recruited me to apply for the position—was afraid I would go into labor if I worked too hard. Before maternity leave, she seemed relatively considerate, did not ask very much of me, and seemed very chill, to say the least. However, I did notice her condescending tone with the team.

She seemed to belittle most people in the office with the questions she asked them and the comments she made about their work. It definitely caught me off guard—not because any of it was directed toward me, but because I had never been in a work environment and seen people treated this way in real life! As a person with high relationship management and social awareness, I study people in social settings. If people are uncomfortable with certain interactions, I will usually pick up on it. If certain people don't click, I'll know. If someone in a group is offended or not connecting with the humor of the conversation, I'll be on alert.

So, as I studied the team during her degrading and belittling treatment, I was dumbfounded that no one seemed fazed. There was nobody shifting, eye aversions, or facial color changes. I was perplexed. My read of the room and conclusion was that this was the "real world" outside of the Liberty bubble. This was just how the work environment was, and I had to get used to it. Nonetheless, I was relieved that I never seemed to be on the receiving end of the treatment. Until I came back from maternity leave, that is.

Back to the "neon Wardlaws." We were building relationships, making connections, and quickly gaining popularity. Since Gary and I had been pretty open and active on social media, it became a mechanism for keeping everyone updated on the East Coast so we wouldn't have to find ourselves constantly on our phones with our family and friends. But it quickly became apparent that, for whatever reason, our acclimation to our new city was going to be another source of insecurity for my new supervisor. Once I painfully learned that she led from a place of insecurity, I understood that those are the most dangerous "leaders" there are. This is especially dangerous in the form of an insecure and violent white woman.

Unfortunately, when you're surrounded by insecurity, whether or not it's racially impacted, you will likely have a difficult time getting encouragement or feeling supported. My earliest lost relationships began while I was still at Baylor—eroded by the acid of insecurity. Kristan was the first.

My law school class was roughly 90 students. Each class was about the same. Anyone who is familiar with law school and the dreaded bell curve knows that it often feels like the Hunger Games. Not everyone is coming out alive, and we all know it. Why do we know? Because they tell you in orientation. And that creates an interesting dichotomy. We all recognize that the people next to you can't survive if you want to make it out on top, but we're all trauma-bonded because we know we're just trying to make it out alive and will likely need one another to do so.

While Kristan was in the class behind me, we had that unspoken trauma bond. To be honest, I remember very little of her in law school. And when I say little, probably nothing at all. But when we met as professionals on the other side, the connection was instantaneous. Working in the field of Title IX during the Obama Administration was complex. It required a very specific skill set (and temperament) to be successful. The learning curve was steep, but the intuition necessary was non-negotiable.

The community was priceless—as well as thirsty—for the connection. No one wanted to be the next school on the Department of Education's "hitlist." And if you were already on the hit list, your misery thirsted for both camaraderie and lifelines. The Dear Colleague Letter of 2011[13] completely changed the landscape of sexual violence on college campuses. The government issued an "advisement" about how higher education institutions were supposed to be responding to sexual violence on campus. The government had essentially identified a shortcut to getting colleges to clean up campuses when it came to sexual violence, and the Office of Civil Rights was policing it.

By 2014, institutions were in a frenzy because of the number of open investigations for the institutions' failure to comply. Needless to say, stress levels were high, and the desperation for camaraderie even higher.

When Kristan and I reconnected as professionals in this field, it felt like a lifeline—a cold glass of water on a really warm day. We were two female Title IX coordinators, not too far removed from law school, at Southern Baptist universities. The connection was undeniable. There was also an added layer of an already complex field. Not only were we navigating the nuances of federal "guidance" (not law) and having to get an entire institution in line with the inferences of said guidance, but we also had to do it at schools that did not believe in talking about sex, let alone assault. Schools run by cultures of religious patriarchy and southern propriety.

We understood one another in ways very *very* few others could.

Now, to say we were chatting on the weekends or texting in between connecting at conferences would be absolutely false. But we would be sure to grab a meal at a conference to take an hour or two to commiserate before heading back to sessions to soak up the knowledge. So to say I knew what was coming when I stepped into her office suite and became part of her team would be completely false.

I was utterly clueless.

And that was a repeated pattern for me. A large part of the grief I feel for the relationships lost, I believe, had to do with the unexpected. I never saw it coming. And I think the thing is, they don't either. Insecurity is a thief. He steals joy, he steals trust, he steals peace. Before a person even knows it, this person you once trusted, hoped, and believed in is no longer for you. They are out to make you look bad, out to elevate themselves, have ulterior motives, and need to be "put in their place."

However, a necessary disclaimer—not every "friend" I lost can be attributed to insecurity. However, one of the major significant factors in unexpected relationship shifts was the presence of insecurity. Kristan was the first to give insecurity a front seat, and before I knew it, insecurity had taken the wheel and had driven us off the road, head-first into a tree.

Sitting in Human Resources being given an ultimatum, one month after returning from maternity leave, after everything I uprooted to do so, still has me in disbelief. And I saw the same patterns over and over again—with every white female supervisor and several peers.

I can say with confidence that Driskell and I never had any type of relationship. She had no interest in getting to know me, understand me, or help me grow professionally. On the two occasions that I recall almost making a connection with her, she quickly sabotaged it. Once when I was about to launch a successful project that typically takes a year, she and the president asked me to complete it in less than three months. Either the Board of Regents or the President's Council had questions about it, and instead of advocating, she abdicated.

"Robyn, why didn't you just let them preview the content?" I desperately queried.

"Oh. I didn't think about it..." she airheadedly mumbled.

The other occasion was when she and I stumbled into discovering that both of our mothers had lupus. It was a real human connection opportunity—one in which it was obvious she was uncomfortable connecting with me about. I'll never know whether it was the subject in general that made her want to move on quickly or whether it was the vulnerability with me. Sadly, I'm willing to bet the latter. Even that brief moment of humanity between the two of us felt unnatural. I believe it was easier to keep me in my relegated position if she continued to remain disconnected from me as a person.

The pattern was no different with her protegee Laura. Once she and Laura were locked in as mentor/mentee, Laura and my relationship began to change dramatically. I do not even know exactly when Driskell determined she was taking Laura under her wing, but I do know I began to sense a shift, and shortly thereafter, Sallie and I began seeing them together—often. Whether it was before or after events that we all were attending, sometimes it was showing up to events together, and my personal favorite—having weekly check in meetings in Laura's office.

The reason that one is my personal favorite is because Laura was a direct report to Robyn, just like Sallie and I. Laura had weekly or bi-weekly update meetings with Driskell, just like Sallie and I. Laura's office was in the Clifton Robinson Tower, just like Sallie and I. But Driskell never made the trip to our office. Sallie and I were expected to travel to Driskell every week or every other week for our meetings. Driskell came to my office *one* time in the years I was reporting to her, which was for a meeting I will never forget (more on that later).

Needless to say, my relationship with Laura changed. The same person who would meet with Sallie and me to get DEI-related advice on her cases. The same person who touted seeing us as her professional peers. The same person who offered to share her Dave Ramsey *Every Dollar* budget sheet password with me so Gary and I could work on knocking out debt the way she and her husband had—later changing the password again to keep me out. The same person who insisted we plan playdates and came to my house with her family for our housewarming was the same person who would eventually tell me I'm "difficult to work with and other [white women] feel the same."

What changed? Proximity to insecure leadership. The thief of trust—a fundamental element of any relationship. The erosion was an avalanche, taking anyone in close proximity in its wake. The erosion ran through HR, taking many of the positive and amicable working relationships I had with that office full of white women with it. But, let's be honest, the retaining walls were weak, so it did not take much. But it was just what was needed to erode what was left of my career at Baylor. Essentially carrying away the Baylor loyalists with it.

Those are the relationships I grieve sometimes. The ones that, at the end of the day, if they have to choose comfort or prestige, career and approval, the known and the accepted, it is a no-brainer for most, if not all. Male, female, black, white, faculty, administration—the "friends" I had to grieve will always choose Baylor.

Part 2:
Reflections Street

September 2018

"It's OK for Black women to 'succeed' within the shadow, but when they deviate, people get a little unraveled." – Dr. Onnie Willis Rogers, Professor of Psychology

Chapter 6: Insecurity Breeds Oppression

One of my kids' latest obsessions is with the movie *Prince of Egypt*. It doesn't bother me because I love the story of Joseph and Moses. Their stories have always resonated with me so deeply—unlikely leaders called to speak truth to power. The theme of stepping out on faith to speak truth to power without fear of the repercussions. My husband even jokes that when he and I get to heaven, I'm going to leave him for Joseph—which may or may not be true!

I also greatly appreciate a lot of these animated movies my kids watch because there are deeply powerful messages—messages I see and hear because the Spirit illuminates them to me. *Prince of Egypt* carries the very overt message of hope and belief in what we can't see and what seems far off. Of course, very inspiring to anyone with a heart. But another glaring message that jumped out to me was the process of how the Hebrews became slaves, why they remained slaves as long as they did, and why Pharaoh made the decision to have the male babies thrown into the Nile.

Because insecurity breeds oppressive practices, oppressive decisions, and oppressive and aggressive violence.

These are the truths that perpetuated violent slavery in America for centuries. These are the truths that fueled the violent demise of the Reconstruction Era, where freshly liberated Black minds and bodies were voted into leadership positions in masses in the South.[14] Only to be violently overthrown and threatened by unchecked lynch mobs.[15]

These are the truths that perpetuated Jim Crow laws and segregation.[16] These are the truths that perpetuate the psychological, physical, and mental/emotional disrespect and abuse of Black bodies today.

There is an unprecedented power that Black folks operate in. The power in our creativity, the power in our minds, the power in our hearts, the power in our intellect, and the power in our resilience.

Pharoah saw a power in the Hebrews that both intimidated him and exposed his deep insecurities. An insecurity that said, "These people are too strong, and I/we are supposed to be the strongest people in the world… what can I do to keep them beneath me? Ah, yes… belittle and subject their minds and bodies to forced labor and strip them of their children—all in an effort to stay in control at the hand of violence."

Who knows the deepest thoughts and chambers of Pharoah's heart, but the connection is undeniable. When individuals represent the power and control in society, their deepest insecurity is losing that power or control at the hands of someone more powerful. In acts of desperation to maintain control, the only way to keep the outside power at bay, is to violently and aggressively, oppress them—mind, body, and soul.

Chapter 7: Sexual Harrassment/Assault v. Racism

Title IX v. Equity

God is so funny. I love the way He works. Now, can I say that all the time in real time? More often than not, no, I can't. In hindsight, His ways can often be seen as beautifully orchestrated and seamless. One of those spaces in my life has been my career path(s). The journey felt painful and chaotic, but in hindsight, it's pure brilliance.

After law school, my mentor and pastor offered me a salaried position as a conduct officer in Student Affairs at Liberty University. This was the perfect opportunity for me at the time. I would have to wait months to get my bar results, I didn't have any law jobs lined up, and my fiancé was in a graduate program at Liberty and would receive tuition remission through me with this job. Perfect short-term gig, right? Wrong.

Gary had a whole year to finish the program, so I needed to stay at least until the summer of the following year. And as "fate" would have it, I didn't pass the bar—*twice*. But as devastating as those results were, in the midst of waiting for the results the second time, I fell for the job.

The following summer, I attended a higher education conference where I was getting a mediation certification, and half the participants in the room were attorneys. I was dumbfounded. I knew why I was there, but I couldn't understand why *they* were. As we spent more time together and I heard more of their stories, I quickly learned that they all wanted to be there. They began sharing with me the quality of life that was available to me as a JD (juris doctor) in higher education. Thanks to that conference,

I made a decision that I was going to be all in for however long I was going to be in higher education.

It was a beautifully twisty and rewarding road that led me down a path of what I dreamed of doing with my JD—advocacy for children. But these children were college students who were just kids trying to find their way to adulthood. My passion for advocacy, specifically for marginalized students, within a few short years, by God's grace, led me to executive director of Title IX at Liberty University. I loved this job. I was in the pocket. I sensed that I was exactly where I was supposed to be, and so did many people around me. It was clear I had a "knack" or anointing to explain to people the nuances of the government Title IX guidance around education system responses to sexual violence/assault, sexual harassment, interpersonal violence, and stalking.

Title IX's primary history was focused around equality for women in sports, but had rapidly evolved in the early 2000s to the role I was now in. Everything about the job came naturally. It was natural for me to speak to an auditorium full of faculty and explain Title IX succinctly and relatably. I frequently answered field questions from aggravated professors who didn't understand why they had to navigate their interactions with students and each other much more mindfully than they had previously done for the last 30 years.

"If a student is speaking with me in confidence about something personal that happened to them, I have to report it?!" they would scoff.

To which I always calmly but confidently replied, "Yes."

It was natural for me to think critically through the details of a complicated case with an investigator who was desperate to consider all sides. It was natural for me to brainstorm fun and creative ways to promote the conversation and raise awareness in a Christian environment without everyone exiting the stage right before they've bought into the vision. And it was natural for me to take the heat, the fight, and the flack from the good ol' boys club at the top of most higher education institutions—especially Southern Baptist ones.

So getting cooperation around programming, funding, and investigation outcomes around sex and relationship violence was a call and an anointing. But it was embedded deeply in my call to advocacy—specifically for marginalized groups. And marginalization of sexual assault victims at Christian institutions is our classic woman at the well—no one wants to touch it until it's trending. I've gone through the fire and fought like hell to normalize the conversation.

And just like that, as soon as my train of acceptance and embrace was just pulling into the station, it was time for me to change trains. The advocacy engine was taking me to DEI, but more specifically, *racism*. I was gearing up for a different fight. Both are steeped in oppression and hiding in the cloak of the brokenness of our society—a society largely dominated and influenced by the Westernized Christian religion, where power and control reign supreme and where keeping the marginalized invisible and silent is the way of the land.

My modus operandi was always a voice to the voiceless. "Speak up for those who cannot speak up for themselves, for the rights of all who are destitute. Speak up and judge fairly, defend the rights of the poor and needy" (Prov. 31:8-9). I carry this with me in all of my work. So it shouldn't have surprised me when the heat seemed even more intense on this new train. Why did it feel like there was even greater offense, even more intense combative responses, or awkwardness around this area? Yet again, I found myself having to have hard conversations about something that wasn't trending, an area that we "just don't have the money to attend to right now" at both Liberty and Baylor.

My passion for this work burned brighter and hotter at Baylor. Because, by this time, my eyes, heart, and mind were opened and exposed to even more injustices that dated back to the fibers of both our country and the church as I knew it. The path was clearer and people needed to be enlightened. And just like that, I was forging a path that did not exist, yet again. Starting over. The heat was hotter and the stakes were higher.

But just as He promised, He had refined and prepared me and us for such a time as this. And what is clear to me in hindsight is God gave us the passion and vision—we were always ahead of the culture. So, the embrace was hard to come by. Suddenly, it was socially acceptable to call out a sexual assaulter, even if he was a priest or leader in the church. But to do the same when it came to racism was and is "unthinkable, "distasteful," "out of pocket," "misguided," or even "malicious."

The way I see it, it's a sin, and it needs to be called out. But before Gary and I knew it, we quickly understood our callings as prophets and realized there was nothing glamorous about being on the opposite side of the societal trend. It's lonely. It can be quite disconcerting—particularly when you're calling it out to people who profess to be a part of "the church." So, the years I spent building, proposing, and advocating were not in vain. They are a part of walking in the call. I now recognize that there's no need to be confounded or perplexed by the social acceptance to address sexual victim marginalization and social rejection of the callout of racism.

***

During most of our tenure at Baylor, we were active members of Antioch Community Church—a church where we grew and built quick connections and relationships similar to Baylor. There were constant affirmations that that was exactly where we were supposed to be at that time. Ironically, we departed in just as much of a dramatic fashion from Antioch as we did from Baylor. It was painful.

The hindsight in the departures is astoundingly clear in many ways. While our popularity and acceptance at both major religious institutions was an enjoyable time, it was never about mere enjoyment. It was always about the will of the Father to get a message to his children. God had given us an undeniable platform, a platform to communicate a message, albeit an unpopular message, but a message nonetheless on behalf of "the least of these" (Matt. 25:40). His children had been marginalized by mainstream society.

And as much as Westernized "Christians" want to claim that we are persecuted and marginalized, the reality is that the Christian religion is the mainstream culture in our country and society. And there are many voices that have been silenced by our mainstream society for a very long time. One of those voices was that of the African American. *But*, there was a shift that was about to happen in 2020—a shift that would not be a surprise to the Father but would definitely be a surprise to the world.

While we were at Antioch, the senior pastor, Jimmy Seibert, spoke often and very emphatically about the kairos moment that was approaching in 2019 and 2020. I can't speak for others, but for me personally, I was ecstatic about this "exciting time" that was coming. Unbeknownst to me, and probably everyone else, there was actually a violent shake-up coming.

This popularity, voice, and platform we had was not coincidental, nor was it for our vain enjoyment. It was for the primary purpose of getting a message to the people. We had the ear of the people. And the Lord knew when he told Brittney and Gary to go, we went. When I tell them to speak, they will speak. So, when it was time, we did just that. And if I haven't learned but one thing since coming to Waco, it's that obedience does not immediately result in feel-good blessings. It does not always mean we experience a happily ever after right away or even on this side of eternity. It also does not mean it will "make sense" to anybody else—even the professing, Christ-following folks.

So, as we found ourselves speaking out aggressively about the systemic racism that we were observing at this mega-church, it did not go over well with those in leadership who felt that they "were so good to the Wardlaws." As if we were doing this from a place of resentment or bitterness. What most didn't understand was this was coming from a position of requiring justice or calling for accountability for righteousness. We knew there was much that had been done in secret in the name of "honor" and it was time to deal in transparency and truth.

One of the pastor's wives had been a mentor of mine since we joined. She made it a point to call me in the midst of all the chaos that ensued in the process of us speaking out. I was pregnant during this time and doing my best to protect my psychological well-being. But our relationship had roots. So, I took her phone call. I do not recall all of the details of the conversation, but I do remember trying to manage my three very rambunctious littles at the time. I felt extremely fatigued at the end of this pregnancy.

She was on the other line gently demanding things like, "Explain what it was that you and Gary are doing. I get doing whatever you are doing against Baylor, but not the church."

"Did you see our video?" I asked her, as I did with most people seeking to understand. I believed she would have the insight and clarity she was seeking after viewing it.

"Yes," she said casually yet matter-of-factly.

I was shocked. Quiet. The realization that this was a dead-end conversation began to sink in. It was becoming clear that, due to the intimacy of our relationship, she was likely sent to disarm Gary and me.

"I don't understand..." she both emphatically and gently continued. At that point, she likely began to further explain why we shouldn't be doing what we were doing, but I think the room was spinning for me at this point. She didn't understand? A Black person whom I had trusted, who had mentored me and walked so closely with me—one whom I had believed to have been walking so closely with the Lord—didn't understand? This fight was more marred than I thought.

She proceeded to caution me and advise me of the potential consequences for "speaking out against 'men of God.'" And with all the calm I could muster, in spite of feeling completely overwhelmed by this call in the middle of my single parenting day, I matter-of-factly queried, "If the pastor was sexually abusing members of the congregation and we were speaking up about it, would you be saying this?"

There was a long pause on the other end of the line. And then a short, "No, that's different."

After that, I knew there was nothing else to discuss.

Chapter 8: Why Don't White Men Bother Me as Much?

It's interesting that I do not have knee-jerk reactions to white men the way I do white women. Why is that? I think, initially, a lot of it has to do with the main implementer of my trauma—it's been at the hands of white women. It's interesting to me when I hear black men close to me talk about "the white man." But as I sat and reflected on it, I realized it reminded me of a scene in one of my kids' favorite animated films—the *Wreck-It Ralph* sequel, *Ralph Breaks the Internet*.

In this particular climatic scene, Ralph has morphed into this enormous mutation of himself. The premise of the mutation is his insecurities about his friendship with his beloved Vanellope. The more insecure he becomes, the more treacherous and destructive this mutation becomes. *Yikes!*

This illustration reminds me so much of many of the white female supervisors that I've had over the years. I'm slowly beginning to understand, little by little, their precarious position to the white man in America. I won't begin to claim that I have arrived at my understanding, but I do recognize that their dynamics at play have directly impacted how they function, survive, and thrive, specifically in corporate America.

However, because of the dynamics at play in the toxic relationship to power between white men and white women, it breeds a uniquely toxic insecurity in many white women to the detriment of the rest of us.

So, while white men have not been the *direct* source of much of my personal trauma, I look to them to recognize that due to the historically poisonous system and position that they've placed their white counterparts in over the centuries, they are responsible for breeding insecurity that has mutated into something lethal and violent—specifically toward BIWOC (Black & Indigenous Women of Color).

Let's consider the historical abuse of scripture to keep women in a subservient position in the name of "submission." An expectation of silence behind or beneath the man, despite God creating *them* in His image, and both being endowed with gifts for kingdom building. One can deduce how suffocating this could be. Not only did we see this play out in the home, but in the church, as well as the workplace. This permutation of the Bible was met with a permutation of personhood and character. We saw this same permutation on the plantation...

How often are the white women in leadership labeled a "bitch" or avoided as someone with whom you would not want to cultivate a friendship? It's the position that many have morphed into in order to survive and thrive. In addition to that, as I mentioned, this evolution was built from a place of insecurity. Insecurity being the foundation of their character—carefully masked as strength or whatever else you want to label it.

The closer you get to the fault lines of this rocky foundation, the more treacherous and even unpredictable they become. I saw this first-hand—over and over again. The more I questioned, critiqued, or innovated in my spaces—getting dangerously close to making them look bad or exposing them as imposters of their competency—the more unpredictable and violent their behavior was toward me.

In one of my first jobs out of college, I reported directly to a white woman. I vividly remember things starting really well but taking a turn within the first six months. Her direct supervisor was a mentor of mine, which was how I initially got wind of the job. I recall her and I having discussions around the directives I was receiving on what to do for each of my cases as a conduct officer in Student Conduct at this university. However, I also remember it being a bit frustrating.

I came into the role thinking that, because I had a JD, this was a space and opportunity to use my critical thinking training. However, I quickly found out that the expectations of this role were not to think at all. We were to receive a directive and execute it. No questioning, no creative solutions, no request for a deeper understanding allowed. Before I knew it, I was receiving a lateral "promotion" with new responsibilities and a new supervisor.

I didn't think my interactions with this particular white woman were hostile or contentious, but a comment in passing by my mentor—who was also the executive supervisor in the department—a few months later told me otherwise.

He jokingly mentioned, "Yeah, if I hadn't given you that role, you and Ashley would have killed each other."

Huh? You mean to tell me that thinking critically and wanting to have a less surface understanding of my job was a merit for imaginary homicides? I was utterly perplexed back then.

Let's fast forward a few years to Kristan–white woman supervisor #2—the woman who recruited me for this particular role at Baylor. Many have asked or thought, "Brittney, if these women are so racist or insecure, why would they recruit you? Why would they advocate for you in these jobs to begin with?" Well, that's easy—they knew me from a safe distance. The kind of distance that makes me look like a shiny new toy or a cute, fluffy-haired pet that's harmless, does tricks, and plays well with others. But somewhere in the intimacy of the working relationship breeds insecurity—kind of like wet wastelands that breed massive, man-eating mosquitos!

I actually remember the first day this particular white woman's toxic insecurity was fed. Gary and I had not been in Waco but a few short weeks. As I mentioned, it did not matter where we were, people were drawn to us. We made friends and built relationships in every direction. Whether it was the grocery store, a sporting event, the farmers market, or a street corner—we literally felt like people magnets.

Like the time I met a professor at the basketball game and the next day he called the Title IX office to make a report, specifically with me. And Kristan asked, with a hint of disdain, "Why is he calling you?"

I had no idea how to answer that. Looking back, these instances are glaringly clear on exactly where the turning point in the relationship began. It didn't help that, on the way to the meeting earlier that day, this supervisor attempted to introduce me to more than one individual who quickly and enthusiastically interjected and said we had already had the pleasure of meeting. So, at the time, my only thoughts and feelings were slight awkwardness and humbled embarrassment.

In retrospect, it brings a lot of perspective to the treatment that followed. Over the next few months during my very short stint under that supervisor, she crafted a malicious and calculated performance improvement plan to get me terminated after only working four weeks in the office, taking eight weeks off for maternity leave, and barely working three weeks after maternity leave.

Both my husband and a dear friend recently made a comment to me along the lines of it being "a miracle that [you] hadn't lost [your] mind or been in a straitjacket at this point" at the thought of working in corporate America at a PWI (predominantly white institution) with a white woman as my supervisor.

Just recounting two of the countless instances of "Wreck it Ralph" syndrome over these last 10 years further solidifies how barbaric and violent these women and their experiences have been. When I first heard the term "violent" used by Rachel Ricketts in her book, *Do Better*,[17] I have to admit, I thought it was a tad extreme. However, as I begin to unpack the events of my experience, I'm realizing more and more how incredibly historical and appropriate that adjective is for the experience of BIWOC, particularly Black women, at the hands of white women.

Chapter 9: ERGs

One of my greatest accomplishments while at Baylor that has catapulted me into quite a few leadership spaces and income-generating opportunities post-Baylor was being a part of the steering committee and executive leadership of the university's one and only Employee Resource Group (ERG).[18] The irony of this accomplishment is that it is also one of my most painful. Every time I did a presentation and shared the value of an ERG with them as an individual and the organization, there was a sting and sickening feeling in my gut that made me want to vomit.

As I've become more and more aware of my body, mind, soul, and spirit, I recognize that my stomach is where *everything* is internalized. So, when I reference vomiting, it's because that's where all my emotions, stress, and pain hide out.

The Black Faculty & Staff Association (BFSA) was nothing short of a masterpiece labored in love for black people, the institution, and the desire to see both be successful together. One of our babies born in the creation of the ERG was the idea to think critically and reflectively on how we could support the administration in moving us forward to support their black students, faculty, and staff. We knew that doing this would ultimately result in great successes across the board for the entire institution.

March 2019 was when we as an executive board decided to work on this project, with Dominque ("Dom") and I at the helm of writing and articulating everyone's thoughts into this letter. Before starting the work on it,

I put my supervisor, the chief of staff (Driskell, white women supervisor #3) on notice that this was a project we were working on.

Dom and I (as president and president-elect), with the help of the rest of the executive board, spent months on this letter, rethinking, rewriting, and reconsidering every element—desiring nothing more than to accurately communicate the sentiment of the black Baylor community at large. The beautiful thing about the executive board is that we had acute insight into every major facet of the Baylor community—from compliance, equity, and DEI to marketing, human resources, the Multicultural Office, and the faculty. The insight and perspective were undeniable.

Baylor did not—until *very* recently—have a single person of color in executive leadership (except two biracial individuals that pass, except when it is convenient to note that they have Native American and Latino in their background). We were all working close enough to someone in executive leadership to know what was going on.

So, what does this letter have to do with ERGs and your point of stomach turmoil, Brittney? Well, let me tell you how the roll out of this letter in September 2019 unfolded. As I mentioned, this letter was very well thought out and revised numerous times– so much so that we set out to write it in March and did not send it to the administration until September. Why do I remember so vividly that it was the first week of September? Because I will never forget the phone call I received the evening of September 4 as we were leaving dinner on our way to drop Anastacia, our daughter, off at Portraits—a children's fine arts program run by the black matriarch of Baylor.

I will never forget that phone call because of the way the white woman supervisor #3 chastised me for the letter. It was a belittling feeling I've only ever felt from a violent white woman in authority who feels threatened in some way and needs to remind me "of my place."

The most potent of those women were my sixth-grade history teacher, my supervisor (the Title IX coordinator, white women supervisor #2) when I first arrived at Baylor, and now this woman. Reflecting on these occurrences, the common theme and feeling that runs through them all was that I put forth my very best work, nothing short of dancing and doing acrobatic tricks for their approval, only to be met with aggressive and violent belittling of my work, efforts, and ultimately heart.

That phone call that is seared in my mind and heart was also the searing point of my career. I knew at that moment that any hopes and desires I had to lead any charge at Baylor University around our equity efforts would never happen. Any hope of an upward trajectory in my career at Baylor had officially run off the tracks, and I knew it. Regardless of the fact that there were six individuals who drafted and signed that letter, I had single-handedly become responsible for what the administration labeled as an "aggressive demand letter" that effectively "blindsided" them. Her words.

The depression and shame I felt were so heavy that I could not even bring myself to talk about it with the board for a couple of days. I sent brief text messages to let them know a little bit about Driskell's response and left it at that. Once I was able to lift my head again, I had a conversation with Dom, who shared with the rest. I cannot truly articulate the shame and heaviness I felt for months. The hopelessness of advancing after working so hard in such a calculated manner. Constantly shrinking and suffocating aspects of myself only to be chastised, belittled, and shamed.

This brings me to why talking and sharing about how the promise of ERGs within an organization is so painful and sometimes sobering. In my presentations, I explain the goals of ERGs, as well as the tangential benefits along the way. Benefits such as demonstrating to leadership your organizational and leadership skills. Providing the opportunity to collectively communicate with leadership so as not to single out one person to articulate the needs of a marginalized group. It is a mechanism to have your knowledge and expertise be better utilized, and also create career promotion opportunities.

I knew these things could and should happen in a healthy institution or organization that genuinely desires cultural equity and inclusion. Even in the post-George Floyd era, Baylor uses that letter as a blueprint for their DEI growth. The same letter was used to decapitate my career, ultimately leading to my resignation/involuntary termination. My silent prayer as I lead these sessions that I now get paid thousands to facilitate is that the listeners are at an organization that supports the healthy, welcomed, and researched approaches to establishing ERGs, ultimately for everyone's benefit—both the marginalized and the organization.

Chapter 10: $125,000

Me, my attorney, my husband, Linda Livingstone, HR, General Counsel (GC), and their new shiny black attorneys from their new shiny black firm.

"Best and final offer. Take it or leave. Sign here. And agree to never apply for a job at Baylor University and agree to never accept a job offered to you by anyone at Baylor University. And agree to never talk about what you've seen, heard, or experienced. To anyone."

Anyone that has been through any type of breakup can tell you that more often than not, there are *many* layers of that breakup. There are details that knit the story, nuances that lead to the build up, and usually the final blowout that seals the deal. I was asked the other day about an aspect of my story that I haven't really spent much time reliving. The "when was it over?" question.

It was the recognized onset of the pandemic in the United States—March 2020. Baylor had just launched a very flamboyant campaign about the expansion of the Equity Office! After months of searching for the assistant VP of equity, they had identified a young Black doctoral student from Indiana. He seemed to have great experience, presented well, and looked the part (non-threatening, conservatively dressed, clean-shaven, light-skinned). All boxes were checked.

The entire Equity Office welcomed and celebrated him with open arms. Who did that include? Oh, forgive me for failing to formally introduce the Equity Office—meet Brittney Wardlaw, the manager of Equity and Civil Rights, recruited by Baylor University to be the deputy Title IX coordinator (Deputy TIXC); later bullied and belittled by the Title IX coordinator (TIXC) after returning from maternity leave, and because everyone was afraid of the windstorm TIXC would cause if chastised for her bullying behavior.

I was removed from the Title IX office, and placed in HR as the sole EEO employees' assistant, three levels below a director without a single direct report—with hopes that I would be content with that because I kept my $90,000 a year. When I'd get anxious about my closet position, they'd tell me how they had big plans for me to oversee equity.

Meet Sallie Black (whom you briefly met earlier), the manager of Affirmative Action and Equal Opportunity, readily available—and willing—to do most things asked of her in HR, even if that meant changing positions a dozen times since she's been at the university.

She recognized her life circumstances limited her comfort or ability to push back, once saying, with tears in her eyes, "I know I'm a 'yes man,' but it's what I have to do right now."

As I mentioned, the entire equity team and the university were really excited about the hope and possibilities of the future. Baylor had finally decided to place a Black professional (outside of athletics) in an executive-level position! Woohoo—*pause*. Before we get too excited, let's not forget Laura Johnson, our newest Title IX coordinator, who had just been promoted as the associate VP of equity *over* our new black executive! Let's read her qualifications.

Let's see, counselor—awesome. Doctorate—great. A dean of students—stellar... but at a small Christian school in Kentucky with less than 1% of the school consisting of minorities. I wonder if they had a D, E, or I office? We'll leave that for intelligent speculation, shall we?

So, let's do a roll call of the Equity Office. We've got Brittney Wardlaw, JD, as manager, Sallie Black, a 20-year HR veteran, as manager, our new assistant VP, and our new associate VP. Pretty stacked. But, hey, we're just excited to have this black man as an executive on paper, with two managers excited to have him! This all goes down in December 2019.

Let's fast forward to the pandemic and give a little recap on relevant context—shut down, everyone's home. This is about the time that performance evaluations (PEs) are due for review with your supervisor. Remember, by this time, I had already approached both my new assistant VP and associate VP to let them know I applied for the AVP position, and I was not given an initial interview—it hurt, but we know I'm resilient.

I'm a motivated team player who is here to support you no matter what anyone tries to tell you otherwise. They showed empathy for my journey, thanked me for my candor, and we moved forward. One of the most difficult things about telling my story is reliving just how maliciously calculated so much of it was—like the time Driskell waited until the eleventh hour to complete my evaluation, knowing she was planning to leave a very poor review with very weak support and justification for doing so.

And eventually my VP HR friend in high places would also turn a blind eye to Driskell's strategy—perhaps it was a collab, perhaps complicity. I'll never know. Eventually, the credible potential witness would turn a blind eye to the abused and the abuser, hoping that if they recuse themselves now, they wouldn't have any blood on their hands later.

By this time, our hopeful black-faced assistant VP had begun to understand the realities around him. He had no power, no authority, no influence and he essentially was losing hope. His equity team (me and Sallie) did our best to motivate, encourage, and ignite something in him every day in hopes of bringing back the sparks of hope he had when he first landed on "Baylor rock."

We never wanted to discourage or add to his frustrations. There were so many people of color who were so hopeful for him, our office, and equity at the university in general that we had seemingly made too much progress to give up—not like this.

Now, we're in a pandemic, working from home—mainly wrapping up investigations and responding to Asian American and Pacific Islander (AAPI) students who are dealing with new harassment due to racist rhetoric around the COVID-19 virus. I made a few pitches for what we could be doing for our Asian student population and was told by Laura Johnson that that just "wasn't where the university wanted to go at this time." In retrospect, it's nothing but the Jesus in me that I was able to make so many pitches and proposals during my time at Baylor–only for my ideas to be dismissed, to be chastised for being too cutting edge, only to later be used or carried by someone else.

The VP of HR, who I once called my friend, used to always complain about her hair falling out. To this day, I don't know if it's something medically related or not, but I cannot help but wonder if it has anything to do with the stress of the dirty work that happened on her watch in that office. If the events that follow do not shock your conscience, then I do not know what will.

***

HR rolled out a program that we'll call "Employee Resourcing" because of the hiring freeze during the pandemic. There were a number of departments all over campus that needed to hire for some positions, but because they could not hire, the university announced there would be other employees who "did not have work right now" placed in those positions. Guess what? I was the very first person placed in a position that was supposed to be comparable to my level of education and work.

However, I was effectively an entry-level administrative assistant tasked with responding to emails of parents looking for their boxed lunches with the Texas Hunger Initiative—onboarded and reporting to a student worker. And here, ladies and gentlemen, is where I got an attorney. Being legally trained, I know how to identify the elements of a constructive termination.

While all of this happened, our assistant VP looked more and more unmotivated. When we confronted him day in and day out about sticking it out, he reassured us day after day, he's not going anywhere. He wanted to finish his doctorate. He moved his girlfriend, and now wife, here, he bought a house, he uprooted his life. He assured us day after day, "I'm not going to quit on y'all," until he did.

Now, Sallie and I had worked in HR—the belly of the beast. I worked there for a couple of years and with her for decades. He didn't have to say a word. The conversation changed entirely. We knew he was confronted with the infamous "PIP," or *Performance Improvement Plan* ultimatum, and he did exactly what I had done as a hardworking, diligent, intelligent, capable black professional.

He said, "I'll do it and do it well." And they did what cowardly, insecure white women in leadership do—regroup and come up with a different deceptive plan to get rid of him. All Sallie and I knew from him, and all he ultimately said when he let us know he'd be leaving, was that he had decided to resign and felt it was best for us all. So, either he has some type of DSM diagnosable disorder[19] that makes him say completely opposite thoughts and feelings within 24 hours, or he was another black professional who wasn't being controlled as planned and would now be sold off the plantation.

So, how did we get to this mediation table where Baylor's best and final offer is $125,000 for me to take, shut up, and walk away? Well, I had reached my breaking point. I ended up with a lawyer who had a disdain for Baylor University, which truly drove him to go for broke. While his drive at times was truly anxiety-inducing and overwhelming, it also forced me to step outside of the Anglo placating of the conflict at hand and go straight for the jugular.

On May 21, 2020, I drafted a letter written to Linda Livingstone (see appendix) and copied all of my "friends" in high places. These are the friends who were constant sources of encouragement for me as a professional, affirming the value I brought to the institution—even going to Driskell on my behalf to advocate for opportunities to shine. These included VPs, AVPs, and other senior-level executives who had often witnessed the maddening experiences I had.

That letter, which was ironically sent days before the world witnessed the death of George Floyd, led me to a mediation table with GC, HR, Linda, and Baylor's shiny new Black attorneys. The angst, the pain, the anxiety, the weight loss, the miscarriage, the deception, the abuse... all of it led me to say enough is enough. I've seen POC after POC in turmoil and angst, abused, overlooked, belittled, paid, silenced, and sent away. And the drive for justice inside of me could not fight for another dollar.

The dollar amount I would need to keep what I've seen and experienced to myself is nowhere near $125,000, and I'm thankful to the Lord for it. The phrase, "And the Lord hardened Pharaoh's heart," kept coming to my mind during this process. For anyone who is familiar with the story of Moses and his petition to Pharaoh to "let his people go," we recognize the implications and the need for Pharaoh's heart to be hardened so that God's glory could be on display.

At the time, I was bewildered as to why Baylor would not be willing to offer more to a black equity officer speaking up on the precipice and wake of the George Floyd "wokeness" title wave. As I mentioned, the righteous anger for all of the bullying done to Staff of Color (and many other marginalized groups at that institution) would not allow me to take $125,000 and be silenced forever.

My story—and many other stories like mine—need to be told. Unfortunately, there are so many who can never tell their stories because they've been sold, but I bought my freedom.

I will not let the price I and many others have paid be in vain.

Part 3:
Rehab Drive

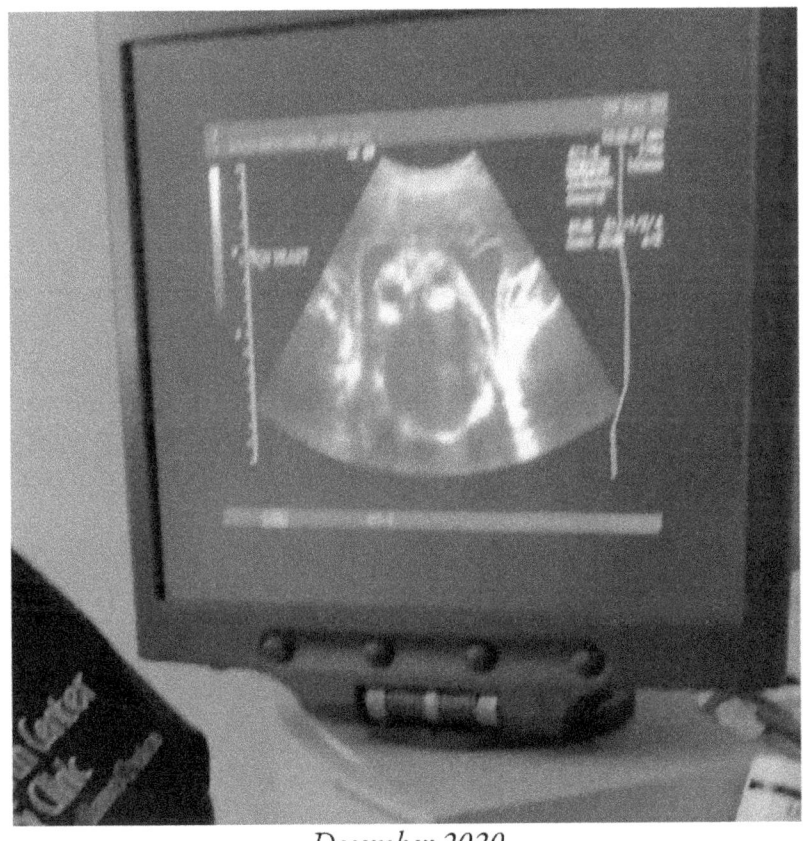

December 2020

Chapter 11: Control

As one can imagine, there were a whole lot of white evangelicals in the Waco community who wouldn't touch the Wardlaws with a ten-foot pole. However, there was a small population of "white evangelicals" that we would call friends who never wavered privately or publicly. Our relationship was driven by something much deeper than any price of losing popularity or status with the community around them. One of our friends who has been there from the very beginning hasn't wavered in making sure our hearts are well and reminding us that this is much bigger than what we all can naturally see.

One of their supportive but challenging notions of pushback was the idea that it's not just about racism and white supremacy in and of itself. They believed this notion or spirit of control permeated the very fibers of these white institutions.

And if I'm being frank, upon first hearing this, I was enraged. Feeling like, yet again, it was white people being dismissive of racism. And what was no shock to me—it was white people we trusted and hoped for something different.

After some time, like many of the complexities and confusion that come with the nature of racism, I was able to sift through and really wrestle with this message. What I realized is that there is something to that statement. For centuries, "Black people" have been innovative, creative, brilliant, resilient, powerful beings who possess a presence that feels threatening to those drunk with the desire to be in control and wield power.

As I reflected on this, it began to make more sense. Was racism and white supremacy a symptom of man's sinful desire to control? Was it the manifestation of creating a hierarchy that required a system of superiority and oppression to control those that feel the most threatening to the power/control that you hold or desire to control?

Ironically, that desire for control and power ultimately caused Satan's demise and the fallen angels that followed! This relentless desire to control is what would drive an entire race to create a system built on the physical, emotional, and psychological destruction of a human life just because there is a desire to control something seemingly more powerful *at all cost*.

So, it appears that my discerning white friends that I was about to cut off may have unlocked something that is critical to understand in calling out and combating this beast of a spirit that has been fed for centuries and centuries!

This is also why we have the compliant house negro. The controlled house negro. And when that house negro is no longer compliantly controlled, he/she quickly finds themselves outside the house or even worse—*sold*. How many of us have been sold? It always looks different. You're offered a severance and an NDA (Non-Disclosure Agreement). You're moved "laterally" on paper, but you know it's nothing short of a demotion. You're placed on PIPs that are impossible to meet when you know the end game is grounds for termination.

We know how absolutely demoralizing this can be because we're all feverishly hard workers, rule book followers, brilliant in our own right, and well-positioned to possibly create real and lasting change or make really meaningful contributions to the betterment of the plantation if taken out of our chains. But most of us are on very short leashes. But if we pull that leash beyond the circumference of where they're comfortable, there are dogs waiting to devour. And these dogs are vicious. Trained to mangle you and dispose of your remains. They clean up as if you never walked the Earth and find the next house negro who fits the part and won't buck the system—until they do.

Is this illustration too graphic for your comfort? Is this not something we're willing to discuss that's embedded in the very fibers of the foundation of how we operate in this country? This is not unusual. But to talk about it makes everyone just a tad bit uncomfortable. Avoidant of any willingness to explore what it means for there to be a reckoning of the process by which the foundations of capitalism were laid.

"*Don't disrupt our system!*" they scream. This is working for us because we've figured out a way to have control of something powerful. The black race. The black female in the belly of the beast that is America.

In May of 2020, America watched as George Floyd lost his life for all to see. It was eight minutes of what black people have been screaming about for decades. What happens to us in the boardroom, in HR, in the hospital, in prisons, in school—day in and day out. And for the first time, in a while, on national television, there was no denying the manifestation of the dehumanization that is black in America.

This was a groundswell that we could not ignore. As we all are very familiar with the Word that says, what is done in the dark *will* come to light. And until we as a "Christian nation" are ready to acknowledge, repent, and lament the foundation we laid, the blood of our ancestors will cry out… Lord forgive them, for they know not what they do. That the very foundations of this nation, the fiber of who we proclaim to be, is built on taking life and, ultimately, control. And the growth of this beast has "shapeshifted" into something no one wants to look at.

But here's the thing… God is a redeemer. Always has been and always will be. But it requires our reckoning and repentance. Until that happens, we can anticipate that this great nation is in danger of being sifted as wheat.[20]

Chapter 12: The Niggers I've Seen Sold

I think a piece of me died every time I watched a black employee get terminated, retire, or "resign." I can't say with confidence that every single black or African American who has left that institution was due to the systemic racism they experienced. However, I can speak confidently of my story and talk about a long list of others that I knew well or had a professional front seat to their tenure and departure.

What is interesting to me is that, when I arrived at Baylor, it seemed every single employee had been there five, ten, fifteen, even over twenty years! I always thought this was a great sign that I could sustain a long-term career. But, in hindsight, these employees were *white*. I hadn't been there long, so it was through casual conversations here and there that I would learn of other Black employees who had come and gone.

It wasn't until I was on my way out that I learned how intelligent, powerful, and influential these employees actually were. They would be casually spoken of in such high regard by black employees, followed by what seemed to be a very reasonable explanation for their departure. Things like her husband got another job, and they moved. Or, she found another teaching opportunity in Dallas. Or, she decided on an early retirement. Seems reasonable, right? Until one stops to reflect on how good Baylor's benefits are, how convenient it is to raise a family in Waco, how well Baylor pays, and how you are pretty much guaranteed a substantial raise every year.

Why leave *that*? Unless you are made to feel you have no choice.

To be honest, that idea probably would have been hard to wrap my mind around had I not experienced it myself. My family and I made a huge leap to be out here in Waco, Texas, at Baylor University. We dove head first. We left everything and everyone behind with very little to fall back on outside of picking up our growing family and making a very costly move back to the East Coast.

So, after my third promotion denial, after having been demoted months after we got here, my senses started to become much more heightened by 2020. I had always been a very trusting person, but since I'd been at Baylor, trusting the system and people to do right by me had left me in a very precarious situation. I had always believed that if I played by the rules, was kind, and worked hard, my story would have a happy ending. But, unfortunately, that's not the way that things play out at Baylor if you're a strong, intelligent, and influential black employee who refuses to conform to white people pleasing and status quo positioning. You will be creatively sold off the plantation.

***

I remember hearing about an attorney, who we'll call Logan, who was employed at Baylor. Allegedly, her last day of employment was the Friday before my first day. I heard repeatedly (from other black employees) how incredible she was. She was dynamic and beautiful and brilliant. Mid-30s, married, with small children.

Aw man, I thought to myself. *I can't believe we missed each other!*

Total happenstance that she was on her way out after a few short years at the institution, right? And total happenstance that she allegedly did not get along with her white female counterparts and supervisor? And total happenstance that she left shortly after being denied a promotion?

There were several others I'd heard about in casual conversation. I was always thirsty to find that black trailblazer to encourage my spirit that it was possible to be black in leadership at this prestigious university. But everyone I heard about was here and gone. There were several others who I wish I knew, but they weren't here long enough for me to get that opportunity. I bought the stories I was told about their departure.

But as my tenure came to an end, and I began to anticipate my departure off the plantation, the narratives about their departure no longer seemed as coincidental or reasonable. There was a theme... An executive director that was retiring early, a few faculty members who found other opportunities, and as I lined up the stories it was starting to make sense—in a *different* way.

There were themes that emerged. If you were highly educated, ambitious, and held your own, typically female, and you usually had some type of friction with a powerful counterpart or supervisor. Even though it's likely deserved, your promotional trajectory will stop in its tracks. And because you know and recognize your worth and can discern things will not get better from here, you make the hard decision to uproot your life and get another job elsewhere because you know your value. *Or* you decide to choose peace and "take an early retirement." They always hold at least a master's degree, but usually a doctorate.

The other theme that emerged is the employee that is more "disposable" and less threatening. Less threatening because the likelihood of their ability (and courage) to cause a ruckus is absorbable. They usually only hold a bachelor's degree, their position is easily replaced, and they're potentially too early in their career to risk being blackballed in higher education. Even though they may feel they've been wronged, they're too afraid to resist and too embarrassed to bring attention to their situation. They are demoted but typically terminated.

No matter which category you fall into, nine times out of ten, you're put on a PIP because HR and the institution need that paper trail to cover their asses.

I lived it. Survived. And then worked in the belly of the beast in HR and had a front row seat, and often a hand, in watching us get sold. I was a house nigger. So I was up close and personal.

Within six months of being at Baylor, they were gearing up to sell me off the plantation. I came in strong, influential, confident, and beautiful. I had made my powerful white counterpart feel threatened and uncomfortable, and they were preparing to sell me. But I was one of the "lucky ones," as they would say. But I know it wasn't luck—it was divine intervention. God, in His sovereignty, knew that I would survive the abuse of the plantation, that I would run away, and I would live to tell my story. With the goal of liberating others—not just the enslaved but the allies as well.

As cliche as it may sound, Harriet Tubman[21] inspired me in ways I never knew were possible. The beauty of her story was not simply that she had the courage to run away but that her rage for what was right and her rage to see others free is what inspired her to continue to fight, even after she had her freedom. She sacrificed a lot. Her marriage. Her family. Her body. For freedom not just for herself but for hundreds of others that she blazed a path for.

Since I've left, I've heard mixed reviews. Those still on the plantation who believe I'm causing trouble, that I "didn't do it the right way," or believe my motives were attention-seeking and self-serving. But I've also heard stories from my white counterparts who also felt inspired and courageous in unexpected ways to go against the grain of a system they knew was toxic and broken. But, I would be remiss not to mention the special few on the plantation who understood what I was doing and quietly encouraged my efforts, assisting me whenever possible, hoping to one day flee themselves.

These were some of the other black and brown faces—many of which, since leaving the institution, are thriving in new working environments. Rediscovering, like I did, that we actually are the incredible professionals that we came to Baylor as and ultimately lost sight of while on the plantation. Others are still there—some grateful for the new power they've been allocated, and some quietly disgruntled but resolved that disrupting the flow of the system is not a risk worth taking.

By the onset of the pandemic, the positive working relationship I had with Laura Johnson had soured. She was operating more and more like Driskell every day. The gold tinsel of Baylor was beginning to tarnish for our new shiny black AVP supervisor. He despairingly realized he had no real power or influence—particularly as he became increasingly frustrated about not being a part of the executive-level equity-related meetings. He was simply another layer between me and Driskell, reporting to two white women who were in charge of DEI for this institution.

We know what happened next. Yep, he was put on a PIP after three short months in the position. And simultaneously, I was the very first employee placed in this "HR program" that was allegedly being used to better utilize university resources. Sallie and I were told that the Equity Office was non-essential and there was little to no work for us to do. Therefore, we would be put in the resource allocation program.

As the typical theme progressed, the new shiny Black AVP was put on a PIP and then mysteriously "resigned." But, they needed at least one face of color in the Equity Office. Sallie was that chosen face because of her very compliant nature, as well as her beloved tenure at the university. And as

I've shared, I was moved into a student worker-level position in a different department.

Now, you tell me what an intelligent, strong, beautiful black employee does in those circumstances? Likely what everyone else like her has done—resign or retire. But as the divine would have it, the fire in me for all that I was experiencing and witnessing would not allow me to be sold—I was running away. And like my respected ancestor, little did I know that I wasn't just running away, never to be seen or heard from again. I was running away and coming back to flip tables.

We're all very familiar with table-flipping Jesus. Has anyone ever noticed in the Book of Mark that Jesus came to the temple and noticed what was going on? He didn't immediately flip the tables. He left and came back and flipped the tables. It wasn't an uncontrolled rage that set in when He saw the corruption. It was a controlled and very intentional rage that He unleashed on His terms—the next day. And when I read that, I realized that not only am I coming back to tell the stories to liberate, but I'm back to flip the tables.

To the ones I saw sold—and especially the ones I stood helplessly by or even helped sell—I am sorry. My heart aches for the pain you experienced and the unexpected rewrite of your story. My prayer is that you have landed on your feet and are prospering. Please forgive me and the systems that have stolen from you. You can stand taller, run faster, and live freer without the baggage from your past weighing you down.

Chapter 13: So What Do You Think of Martin Foster?

A question I am frequently asked is, "What do you think of the chosen black face of the university? The individual that leadership has collectively decided will check all the boxes. The intelligent and articulate negro who will be versed enough to seamlessly navigate executive white spaces without pushing anyone's buttons of discomfort. The name/face they can flash in emails and on board reports to possibly keep the black employee coalitions and the student unions placated and can represent the university well when we need to talk about "black" things.

Someone who is vested enough in their career progression not to compromise their leverage and position for the greater good of the black community. But someone with a kind enough heart that even if they feel like a sellout in any way, they will remind themselves that what they are doing is ultimately for the greater good of everyone. And they have just what it takes to do it well—in spite of the fallen people before him/her. They are convinced that they are different. They've got it figured out in a way that the fallen others did not.

So what do I, as a once chosen and now "fallen" one, think of someone like Martin Foster? Well, for one, I have no desire to malign the Martin Fosters. They genuinely believe they will be the one who makes the difference. And that hope is admirable. That hope is necessary for us, as a people, to carry on the fight for equity and, ultimately, equality. My perspective holds two sides of one seemingly juxtaposed but very synchronized coin. I think at the heart of the question, people want to know—is this individual OK? Is he a sellout? Do you approve of him, what he's doing, or what he will do?

I do think a complex but necessary perspective that the 'Martin Fosters' need to keep a healthy position with the plantation owners is that, *You are replaceable.* When you don't operate as if there are many who have gone before you and many more who will come behind you, you have elevated yourself to a position of pride that inevitably ends with a fall. And it's likely that if you have managed to avoid that fall indefinitely, you have to ask, at what expense have I become a sellout?

Keep in mind what the Bible explains in Ecclesiastes about seasons. No season is forever (Ecc. 3:1-8). The other side of this coin that we have to hold simultaneously is that if we are vested in the work of equity, are we equally vested in doing it the Lord's way? Not in a quiet, complicit, do what I'm told, don't make anyone uncomfortable, Western Christianity way—I'm talking about hands up, blind faith, 100% surrendered to obedience type of way! That living in the woods, eating locusts, and honey radical faith that has people wondering if they need to lay hands because a spirit is in them or if they need a psych evaluation!

When you're living like that, and you're in an ideal career, making good money, in a comfortable small city community, and the Lord says, "Blow it up. Now," you do it. And when he says, "Peace be still. This is where I have you, and this is what I would have you to do." You do that. Nothing more. Nothing less. And you pray for those He's leading with grenades, and you pray for those He's sitting with in enemy camp breaking bread. You pray for wisdom, courage, discernment, boldness, insight, conviction, enlightenment, and peace.

So whether the Martin Fosters are right or wrong, that's between them and the Lord. But they're replaceable. We all are. In a very practical,

"They'll get a new black face if they need to" type of way. But also in a "Do you want to be a part of the Lord's plan or want someone else to get that opportunity?" type of way as well. But, my prayer and position is that we are obedient to the post assigned and willing to walk away when our general gives the orders.

Never operating in a posture of pride that inhibits us from seeing how the sacrifices before us were not in vain.

Chapter 14: When the Two-Step of Their Deception Gets Tangoed

It was a sunny Spring day, and Driskell had her assistant contact me to schedule a meeting in her office. It was just me and her, which was highly unusual. Unless it was performance evaluations, rarely ever did she meet with just me apart from Sallie. We literally did everything together. It was a natural groove that we had fallen into.

One reason is because we genuinely enjoyed one another's company. But also because, when they created my job description, every descriptive line of the job began with "assist with." Hence, all of the work that Sallie and I were given in EEO/HR, and now in equity, was meshed. Needless to say, I was very surprised to have a meeting scheduled with Driskell alone.

I do not remember much about what I was wearing that day, how my hair looked, or even what day of the week it may have been, but I do remember not feeling any sense of nervousness going into her office that day. I had no reason to be concerned. Sallie often encouraged and applauded me for my ambition—often going the extra mile with proposals, projects, and initiatives. As a single mother, she understood her capacity and was always so encouraged that I had a supportive husband who could pick up the slack at home if I needed a little extra support to invest in the job. So, arriving in Driskell's office that day felt different.

It wasn't a long meeting, but it felt life-changing. She shared with me in that meeting that the university had decided to move forward with hiring an assistant VP of equity. This was literally the position I had been waiting for since I began my career in civil rights-related matters before arriving at Baylor University. You see, this was a position that I had proposed at Liberty. One I was told they weren't ready for until a year later when I was putting in my resignation, ironically.

This was a position that I proposed to Baylor HR when they wanted to keep the peace in Title IX during my departure and asked me, "Is there *anything* else at the university that you would like to do?" This was the position that Cheryl Gochis sat with me at a table in HR and looked me square in my eyes, told me she asked Reagan Ramsauyer for the resources to create, and said she and her minion Becky Ivy just needed a few weeks to work out the details but could have me in, and housed in HR. This was the position that even after waiting in HR for a year and a half for this alleged position, I was told they would be using a search firm to fill it—that was in January 2018.

They did at least give me the courtesy of inviting me to the first-level participation—that time. That first-level participation included submitting a series of questions that felt like they had been written specifically for me. Every facet of what they were looking for in this position I had experienced, expressed passion in, and had a vested interest in seeing it come to fruition. So much so that, ironically, this big-time search firm was hitting a major rut in recruiting. They just weren't pulling the individuals that they thought would or should be in this position. This big-time search firm needed some help. So what did they do? They reached out to their big-name people in the world of equity—hoping these big-name people could give them some big-time referrals.

And you'll never guess what happened. That's right—they reached out to my professional mentor, and guess what he told them? You have a solid candidate right there in the university. Her name is Brittney Wardlaw. But I'll hit you with the headlines on how that opportunity played out.

1. I do not get an interview.
2. They bring in three candidates.
3. Nice candidates that no one is impressed by.
4. I'm constantly confronted by my peers, asking what I thought of the candidates and why I didn't apply.
5. The university calls it a failed search, the position is gone, and everyone goes on with business as usual.

So, let's jump back to that Spring day in Driskell's office. Only a few short months prior to this moment, right after coming back from maternity leave with my third beauty, the Lord had dropped a brilliant idea in my spirit that I proposed. This idea is based on an executive-level position focused on alternative dispute resolution. An opportunity for students (and employees) to resolve contentious claims related to Title IX and civil rights through alternative means—namely, restorative justice and mediation.

I have years of experience, worked as a trainer and coordinator at my previous institution and essentially I'm well positioned to create a long overdue functionality of the Equity and Title IX Offices. This is January 2019. Driskell enthusiastically responds, "What a great idea!" And then asks, "Is there any way you can do this without additional funds? We just don't have the money in the budget for this."

In other words, figure out a way to implement what you can as you are because you're not getting a promotion, and I'm not giving you any money to make it happen. Six months later, a peculiar thing happens. Laura Johnson (the white, future associate VP of equity) flies restorative justice trainers to the university, inviting campus partners to be a part of implementing restorative justice and launching an alternative dispute resolution project for the university.

The fact that I was feeling hopeful sitting and leaving her office that day is a testament to the Holy Spirit inside of me. I can honestly say I had some dark days, but there was always hope on the horizon. I vividly remember writing feverishly on my notepad that I brought with me to any meeting—it didn't matter if it was a meeting with the exterminator. My trusty notepad was right beside me. I wrote my meticulous chicken scratch, reviewed it obsessively. Added notes to my notes, thoughts to my questions, comments to my thoughts. I prepared in any way I knew to prepare for a position that seemed like it was calling me, written for me, and after a hard-fought few years of being overlooked for my efforts at Baylor, would finally be availed.

But we all already know the end of this once hopeful saga. This time, I would not get an initial bite. There would be no initial interview. I would be a part of the interview process, but not as a candidate—because it "was only right they invited me in." Truth be told, these interviews did not get any easier. But I had always resolved to participate with grace, class, and decorum. Even when tempted to do otherwise, I was encouraged by just the right person to be true to who I am. And I did exactly that. Even if I had to interview a white woman who allegedly didn't want the position, had no experience in D&I, and used a project I proposed, which she executed, to boost her resume for this position.

But Brittney, wait. Why are you assuming she didn't want the position? Perhaps because, a year earlier, when she came for the Title IX coordinator interview, the Uber driver (who was part of this small Waco town) heard her comment on the phone that "this place was a hard no." And in small-town Waco, he didn't hesitate to pass along what he heard. This is the same white woman who told her team she was approached multiple times by executive leadership to apply for the AVP of equity position. The same white woman that countless individuals on the interview committee came to me questioning how she could be a competitive candidate with "Carson."

Well, the truth is, she actually wasn't. She was *the* candidate all along.

Deception gets messy. It often takes a lot of work and effort to keep all the pieces aligned. I think that's one of the many reasons the Bible says, "The truth will set you free" (John 8:32). Lies inevitably ensnare and indict us. There was another white woman working in my office at this time. Someone I would have called a friend. She was intelligent, pragmatic—rarely engaged in any conversation about feelings and rarely in a conversation that required an emission of empathy. It's almost as if she thought that feelings don't *really* matter.

As an attorney, I'm used to these types of people, so it wasn't anything that shocked me by any means. There were times over the few years we were friends when I would share small pieces of my frustrations with my professional challenges at Baylor. In spite of her career working with marginalized populations, I never overshared because I never felt confident that she was someone who truly sympathized with what it meant to be a black professional at a white institution. However, it was undeniable to most, if not all, of our office mates that Laura Johnson did not fit the bill of what many of us had hoped would be the new face of equity for Baylor.

This friend was familiar enough with my background, my journey, and my heart to know that I would be deeply affected by this decision and announcement. After the news dropped, she would step out of her comfort zone and into a deep feelings situation, coming down to my office to ask me how I was doing. And for the years we had known each other, the lack of emotion on display at my doorway, combined with the devastation I was feeling, was stomach-churning. At that moment, I vividly remember feeling like I wanted to vomit. But instead, I returned the same stale lack of emotion and said, "I'm fine." And with that, she left.

Sometime later, I believe in a genuine effort to console, this "friend" emphatically shared the gory details of how embarrassed Laura Johnson (and rightfully so) appeared to be when she let her team know she would be applying for the AVP of equity position. She proceeded to share that Laura said executive leadership approached her three times, pleading with her to apply for the position of which she eventually conceded.

I think for many POC, specifically Black women at PWIs, the deceptive tango is exhausting. The rhythm and rules are always changing. They're speaking a language we sometimes can't interpret, they're bringing in players and pieces we didn't know were included in the game, and then they're ripping off pieces of the rulebook, throwing them away and penalizing us for not playing correctly. Especially when you feel like you have to learn the steps of this tricky and deceitful dance—because if you don't, it feels like not only are your hopes of thriving slim, but your hopes of surviving are just as bleak.

So, how do we keep in step when we were raised to work hard, do our best, put forth 110%, be direct, honest, and told everything will work out? Many of us have learned the hard way in this deceptive tango that it doesn't exactly work like that. And if we do successfully learn the steps, did it come at a cost? Are we too trading in our honest and straight forward two steps for a deceptive tangled tango?

A disclaimer—many of my experiences are uniquely slimy to white southern Baptist corporate America culture, but some are very generic to the white corporate America experience. However, one aspect of what makes my Baylor experiences unique is that, much like America in general, we have a façade to uphold. That requires a more complicated dance to do sneaky and deceptive things but still look nice and polite along the way. It's gross but oh so real.

In sharing my experiences, I want everyone to know and understand that this is and always will be something much deeper than a rant. Experiences like these have sent POC, Women of Color, into deep places of turmoil and depression. Questioning their competency, their work ethic, their abilities, their value, their calling, their purpose. But the reality is—it's not us. Never has been. But sometimes, when we're so deeply entrenched in garbage, we can't see the horizon or the sun. We lose our bearings and our perspective.

For me, it wasn't until I got out that I was able to get my footing again and remember that I'm a badass—an anointed, gifted, *skilled* badass who lives with great purpose. For some, I am sounding an alarm, and it may be time for you to get the f--- out of there! For others, you're going to stick it out—whether you have to or just want to, there is no shame in either. But what you will know, going or staying, it's not you. Hear it from me—*it's not you*.

You weren't meant to play this game because you're above this game. So don't feel down on yourself if you haven't mastered the steps of the deceptive tango. I'm here to remind you which way is north and remind you of the beat of that two-step sista.

You got this.

Chapter 15: The Day I Felt Molested

As I've referenced, there were multiple instances of job searches for an executive-level equity position that I never hesitated to enter in the running for. I will provide a very clear and succinct timeline of why these positions and the way that they played out were each so deceptively manipulative and devastating. Nevertheless, the last and final time that Baylor made moves to fill the position occurred in November of 2019. This was an extremely eventful time in my career as I made monumental strides forward and backward.

This particular situation occurred the day Driskell made a trip to the administrative building across I-35 to meet with my coworker and me about the outcome of the interview process with the two final candidates for the AVP of equity. This was the first time in the two years I had been working for her that she had ever come to our space. We met weekly, but each week my coworker and I were summoned to her office to meet and provide updates on what we were working on.

On this particular occasion, she communicated that she would be coming to our office space. The three of us met in the conference room and listened to her weave her story about how the decision was made for the position. Carson was a young black man from Indiana with a Master's degree and extensive experience in the DEI field. Laura Johnson was the current Title IX Coordinator with little to no experience in DEI but was clearly the favorite candidate for several reasons—like her white female connection and like-mindedness to the current President's Council, along with Driskell's very obvious mentoring relationship with her at this point.

As I mentioned, in an effort to be transparent with her team, Laura Johnson disclosed that the "leadership" had approached her several times to "highly encourage" her to apply for the AVP of equity position. After making the mistake of communicating with my colleague and me previously about her lack of experience with DEI work and field, Laura was suddenly interested in pursuing the position.

So when she and this young professional from Indiana were the finalists, it was a no-brainer for everyone. Now, before you ask, Brittney, that seems a little biased, doesn't it? I'll beat you to explaining why it's not.

Driskell and her co-manipulators had assembled a dream team of interviewers. Anyone and everyone who would touch anything related to equity in their work was asked to be on these very robust interview panels. However, what Driskell and her squad failed to recognize is that their "dream team" were people who I had worked in very close proximity with, was highly respected by, and who were also highly perplexed about why they were not interviewing me. How do I know this? Because they were calling me!

If there were fifteen to twenty people interviewing, nine to eleven of those people were making efforts, whether in person, by phone, or by text, to understand why I wasn't being interviewed and then what I think they should do or say on the feedback form for the candidates.

Well, I did not hold back. But I did try to be kind and tactful. I communicated that it was obvious to me that Laura Johnson was there because she was Robyn's protegee, which was concerning to many of the people on these interview panels because many of them had articulated at length their frustration with Driskell due to her lack of competence in any of our fields. The other matter that concerned many was that they were looking to hire another white female to oversee the area of equity.

"Brittney, what should we say? You tell me what to write [on the feedback form]" is what I heard over and over again.

And over and over again, I said, "Carson has the experience we need to move the work forward. Laura has leadership experience and has done a great job leading Title IX, but she has little value to add to the equity space."

Now, I recognize that I don't know what people ultimately put down on their papers because everyone was always very good at being *Baylor nice*. However, I do doubt that what Driskell shared in these meetings was consistent with what I was hearing from my counterparts after the interviews.

So we're sitting in this meeting room, and Driskell proceeds to share with us that, "We got really positive feedback for both candidates. So what we've decided to do is hire Carson as the assistant VP of equity [yay!] and promote Laura to the associate VP of equity [huh?!]." It was *the* classic, record-scratching moment. I think the blood stopped flowing to my brain, and I may have momentarily blacked out. My mind was on a midnight train to Georgia! There was absolutely no way I was hearing what I was hearing!

Mind you, I had no professional bones with Laura prior to this process. Her and I had always gotten along great. Her family had been in my home, we had very productive, amicable and pleasant meetings together. So nothing about this was personal. Now, I do question her integrity after she made the decision to apply for the position after having articulated on multiple occasions her deference to me and my colleague on all matters of DEI because of her admitted lack of competence.

The other jaw-dropping reality that was fueling my runaway train was that less than nine months prior to this moment, before the publication of the resurrection of this position, I had very recently prepared one of many proposals and provided it to Driskell for review—the one that focused on building the restorative justice and alternative resolution arm of both the civil rights and Title IX areas. Something no one at the institution had any prior experience with but me.

When I provided Driskell with the proposal she was thrilled about the concept and explicitly communicated that she loved it. However, her follow-up was very pointedly, "Is there a way you can execute this in your current position? Because there is no budget line or funding for another position." Deflated, but committed to trying to remain hopeful, my colleague and I did what we could as an office of two with no authority or team.

So, for her to sit across from this table and articulate that not only were they going to hire Carson in this VP-level position, but they now had the budget for an elevated VP-level position for Laura Johnson to oversee both Title IX and equity as well as this black, experienced, new hire, was enough to run my train into the side of a mountain. But it was these occurrences and many others like them where I repeatedly chose to keep my composure and believe that my integrity, reputation, and work ethic would advocate for me eventually.

Following that meeting, Driskell decided to "visit with me" since she had never seen my office in the two years we were working for her. She came to the doorway, lingered for a bit, and then slowly made her way into my office. She never sat down. And to be honest, I don't know that I can recall whether I invited her to do so. I just remember the interaction being so awkward and forced that I could not tell you anything about the exchange.

I do remember that her 6'3" presence and noncommittal visit felt very unnatural. She slowly eased her way into my tiny office, where I had a small but bulky round table to my back, in between my desk and the doorway. She looked around as if to say, "Well, this is quaint," but made no comments about anything she observed.

Now, I never considered my office private. But it was sacred. It was a place of respite, of worship through my ideas and brainstorming process, of regrouping and meditating. It was a place to house my family for short visits, to gaze and pray as I looked out the window, to eat and rejuvenate. It was also a place to pump milk tirelessly in order to maintain my motherhood desires and responsibilities, all the while sustaining my family financially. It also housed great brainstorming conversations with coworkers, as well as a quiet place to hold some of the deepest heartaches of those coworkers who trusted me.

As Driskell sauntered into my office unannounced and uninvited, there was a slight sense of violation I was feeling. This woman was a deceiver, a manipulator. She had no interest or desire to advocate for me or anyone like me. And now she had the audacity to darken my doorstep as she did not and had not demonstrated any common interest in the things I was passionate about—advocating for the marginalized or fighting against injustice.

As you may recall my experience at the Kirk Franklin concert that same year she had questioned my integrity and accused me of reporting Baylor for embellishing information for the diversity award, also known as HEED. Ironically, someone at Baylor had felt compelled to report the lies to that board—to this day, I have my suspicions, but I have no idea who it was!

Her presence, to say the least, was not welcomed in my sacred space. Was I recovering from the news? Absolutely. But the humbled and belittled position that she had made our relationship made her unwelcomed and towering presence that much more potent. It was a reminder of how little power and authority I had or would be awarded under her watch. So as she made her way into my office, my discomfort grew.

Is this what it feels like for someone to enter into your space uninvited and unwelcome? This is not to minimize in any way the very real and very traumatic experiences of sexual harassment and sexual assault victims, but having worked so closely with that marginalized population for so long, the deep empathy I was feeling at that moment was palpable. Everything in me was crying out for her to leave, but very unsure about what was going to happen next.

As she took her slow steps into my office and looked around without really saying anything, she then took another step toward my sacred table. On that table sat my books. All of the books that I had been deeply diving into over the years to enrich my understanding, specifically of race equity and anti-racism. On the top of the stack was Austin Channing Brown's *Black Dignity in a World Made for Whiteness*. She picked up the book without saying a word, rubbed the front and back as she read the title, and silently put it down, leaving moments later.

The violation I felt at that moment was unexplainable. I was stunned. Why did she think it was okay to come to my office? Why did she think it was OK to walk in uninvited? And why did she feel it was appropriate to pick up a book off my desk and put it back without a wince? As I mentioned, if there was any conversation, it was trivial and brief.

It was such a painful reminder in that moment of who holds the power and the expression of both her conscious and unconscious beliefs of her access and authority over this little black girl who should be grateful she has a job at Baylor University. As I think back on various life-changing interactions like these I had at Baylor, it illuminates for me that I am not the same person now as I was then.

I have grown in ways that I can't even begin to articulate. I recognize how differently I would respond and react now to those situations. It doesn't make me angry thinking about those differences. It actually deeply encourages me. I am overwhelmingly grateful for the growth, the insight, the liberation, and the power for which I am now walking. And I desire the same for all of us. It is God's desire for all of us—liberation and power, freedom and authority.

Part 4: Recovery Circle

September 2020

Chapter 16: Light and Dark

Liberty University has gotten a really bad rap here recently. Our president and founder's son was exposed. The standard of the university was found to be inconsistent with his lifestyle. Much like Baylor, Jerry Falwell Jr.'s dirty laundry was aired on a national level—first on season three of a podcast entitled *Gangster Capitalism*, released in 2021, and then again on a Hulu documentary entitled *God Forbid: The Sex Scandal That Brought Down a Dynasty*.

Unfortunately for the university, all of Falwell Jr.'s indiscretions were connected to Liberty and its now tainted reputation. Leaving a black eye on the legacy of the institution. People have come out of the woodwork to ask me my perspective on Liberty—specifically on the sexual assaults and alleged culture of sexual harassment.

When asked, I told numerous reporters, as the former Title IX coordinator, "I don't think I have the information you're looking for to support the narrative you're writing." As a former Title IX coordinator and an executive mid-level employee, I fought a lot of battles. But, appropriately addressing Title IX related reports (2014 to 2017), was never an issue.

I often had to fight with the good ol' boys club to do things the way I knew they were best, but this was typically a power struggle—not because anyone was trying to cover up indiscretions. *Disclaimer: Getting HR to be transparent about employee-related matters was an impossible struggle.* The more I demonstrated my competence, the more they would bring out the big guns to prove they were on top of things. They went as far as to bring in their external counsel by the name of King Tower to demonstrate his "knowledge of Title IX." It was laughable. It was clear he recently had someone do some research on it and was teaching himself 48 hours before our meetings. But I digress.

Some of Liberty's top-tier leadership has always smelled a little funny, and you could tell who was really about that Christian life and who was a generationally wealthy, born and bred, good ol' boy Southern Baptist who refused to be crossed. But many employees across the university loved them some Jesus. This is why people were OK with making pennies in the name of serving and helping for the greater good. It was exploitation, no doubt, but people had joy. Generally, their lights shone. And we shined alongside one another. At least, that was my experience in Student Affairs. You could tell when people's flesh and egos got the best of them, but there was more light than dark. Dark was the exception, not the rule.

When I found myself at Baylor University, I truly experienced a culture shock, which may seem reasonable considering a move from Virginia. However, the culture shock was truly not for reasons one might expect. Now, when it was happening real-time, I didn't understand the what and why. But now that I've had the experiences I have, it seems painfully and disgustingly apparent.

In my first month in the office, it did feel a little awkward which I didn't think was completely unreasonable being I was in a new place, in a new role. But, it was almost as if my office mates were awkward with me. People were nice, but there didn't seem to be much bonding going on. I worked in the office for a month before I went on maternity leave.

While on leave, Gary and I had a much smoother postpartum than our firstborn, so we were making moves to get to know our new home. We visited sites, took tours, attended events, and made connections. And because our family and friends wanted updates every other day of what was happening, we had made a decision to vlog our happenings on YouTube and other social media platforms so everyone could have access to all the updates in real-time. It was cleaner, less time consuming and everyone could choose to be in the know on the Wardlaws in Waco. Unbeknownst to us, as I mentioned, my new boss was watching as well. Again, these are not things I knew in real time, but I clearly gained access to them over the months and years that followed.

I took maternity leave for what ended up being eight weeks (because I ended up getting the stomach flu toward the end and had to take an extra week). When Baylor hired me, I asked explicitly if I would have full benefits for maternity leave, but they didn't tell me that there was a no paid leave policy. I moved my family of four across the country, eight months pregnant, and was unpaid for those eight weeks.

The workplace abuse started when I tried to come back early. My supervisor Kristan told me that she and Becky Ivy, her HRC, determined I couldn't come back until the date we all agreed upon. We had no money to put our daughter in school, we were still paying on our mortgage in Virginia. We were at the point of asking friends and family for $50, $100 just to make ends meet.

And when I asked if I could start working, she retorted, "Is this financial?"

I was taken aback by her invasive question, but I shamefully replied, "Yes."

To this day, I'm so thankful for people like my mother-in-law, my friend Robin, and our friends Nikeya and Jarel, who were not living in abundance by any means but felt led to send us money. Gifts that usually brought us to tears because they were given with no strings attached because they felt led.

Once I returned to the office, it was incredibly difficult. The verbal abuse and humiliation I experienced at the hands of my supervisor was debilitating. She would scold me for speaking with my colleagues or office consultants about my projects.

"I expected you to be more competent... you have major gaps in training." She wanted me to isolate myself. Her insecurities were requiring her to make sure those around her felt less than. And it was working. I had never been treated like a dog in the workplace up until this point. And everyone seemed unphased. I'm not sure what disconcerted me more—the ill-treatment or the complete "walk on the opposite side of the road" behavior of the team. No one spoke up. No one interjected. No one came to my office to reassure me that I wasn't losing my mind. Literally no one.

Obviously I had been talking to Gary about everything every day. But after about a week or two I had started to confide in the Spirit led people in my life. One of those people was my brother and dear friend PJ.

The conversations wouldn't be long, but long enough for me to give him a few updates so he would know how to pray for me. I will never forget one brief conversation we had one day when I was in the office. I think I was in a conference room alone and I was sharing briefly what I was feeling and experiencing.

"I'm just confused, bruh. I literally don't feel like I'm doing anything right."

He said, "You're light, Britt."

"What do you mean?" I replied. My understanding was I was recruited from my Christian university to another Christian university to help them do the right things. I had experience and Christian higher education experience. I was perfect for this role. I'm coming from a Christian environment and going to a Christian environment... right?

"They don't like the light, Britt. It's like roaches scattering. You've stepped into a dark, dark space, and the darkness is trying to recalibrate and get you out. Don't give up, Britt. It's nothing but spiritual warfare."

What?! I was totally and utterly confused. My mind was completely blown. I couldn't even compute what he was saying. How could I be at a "Christian" school and be the light in the darkness?

Human Resources ends up "doing me a favor," and getting me out of Title IX with Kristan and moving me to HR where I could "be over equity." Every Friday, we would huddle. The themes would change, but we always had Friday huddles nonetheless. During the Thanksgiving season one year, the team I was a part of was responsible for leading it every week that month. During my week, I shared Philippians 4:6-7. I remember this huddle so vividly because I always remember those moments when the Spirit speaks powerful truths through me.

I shared about some of the power of those verses—particularly how with "Be anxious for nothing but in everything by prayer and supplication *with thanksgiving* we are to let our requests made known unto God, and the *peace of God*, which surpasses all understanding *shall keep your hearts and minds* in Christ Jesus!" I emphasized the key is "with thanksgiving." When we're postured there, our anxiety subsides, and the Spirit of the Lord does what He does in our hearts. Listen, I was preaching! Enthusiastically! And let me tell you, the room was unmoved. It felt incredibly awkward and tense.

I can't say I've ever experienced anything like that. I had numerous opportunities to "share" at Liberty and I was usually the only woman in leadership doing so. And every time, the crowd was locked in. People would come up afterward to tell me how it moved in their hearts and spoke to their souls! Now, let's be clear—I never shared with an expectation of accolades or compliments, but mainly for the Spirit to show up and people not to walk away the same. But when I say it was weird and awkward, I could have crawled under the rough, glued carpet and stayed there until the cleaning people came that evening. Yet, I was still confused.

As the months in HR went on, I made lots of... frrrr...enemies. For every "friend" I had in HR, I had three enemies. The more I presented ideas to navigate conflict or keep people accountable for addressing the issues of the marginalized, the more I made frenemies. I even remember when they threw me a mandatory baby shower—it was awkward, I don't think people wanted to be there, it was only celebratory because one of my only friends in HR (Sallie) was the one that threw it. These people tolerated me. They weren't celebrating me by any means. They could fake the smiles, but I felt it and chose to be as genuine as possible in spite.

One day when I was still in the Title IX Office, we went to a luncheon shortly after I returned from leave. I can't recall if it was for someone's birthday or if it was a going-away luncheon for a team member. I specifically remembered it was at Ninfa's, a popular Mexican food restaurant in Waco. Good food, lively culture, and good vibes. A pleasant outing for a team, friends, or even a date.

I remember the conversation at some point turning to me about Gary and me and our vlogging life. We had taken to vlogging while I was on maternity leave, which is why Kristan knew so much about us making the most of our leave and getting to know our new town! Vlogging was our anecdote to the countless calls and text messages we were getting from family and friends wanting updates about the move, details about our transitions and circumstances, assurances of our financial well-being, etc.

So we decided, instead of spending countless hours on our phones, we would vlog so everyone could have the updates at once if they were interested! Unbeknownst to us, this was a practice that would translate into showing and inspiring people about the journey of walking in faith—the good, the bad, and the beautiful.

I believe someone at the table made a positive comment about it and there was some laughter and smiles about the content they had viewed. But the conversation quickly took a turn. Kristan and her minion Mike (I call him a minion because he was the one white man in the office who echoed and signed off on anything she said or directed before she even completed her thoughts) decided to question and lecture me about said vlogging.

"Do you think it's safe to put information about yourself and your family on the internet like that?"

"Yeah, I never share anything personal about my life on the internet."

"Yeah, the nature of what we do could really be endangering…" And the barrage seemed endless. The more they talked, the more my heart was beating out of my chest. The anxiety was coming over me like a title wave. There were so many thoughts that were running through my head and so much humiliation I was experiencing at the moment—all eyes were on me, and all I felt was embarrassment, and no one at the table, yet again, had anything to say.

I left lunch pretty devastated and anxiety-ridden. I couldn't go home and tell Gary not to vlog anymore. This was a hobby that was sustaining him emotionally and psychologically. It was giving us both joy in a foreign land, keeping us connected in a way that we desperately needed right now. And at that moment, my phone rang. It was our former pastor, friend, and mentor, Keith Anderson. He had no idea how timely that phone call was. I word-vomited on him about all that had happened at lunch, how I was feeling, and desperately sought his counsel.

He calmly replied, "Britt. I'm the dean of students. No one has had harder conversations and more difficult interactions with students and families than I have. I am unapologetically on social media. And I know what I'm using it for. I have never in all of my years had any issues with *anyone* that I have had to interact with. And you know why?"

With tears in my eyes, I quietly replied, "Why?"

"Because you and I know how to treat people. When you see people and treat people for the human beings they are, with care and compassion, you can literally change the course of their lives with one decision, and they leave respecting you and feeling cared for. You don't have to worry about what they were trying to project on you, Britt. You were the director of Title IX. People left your office the same way. Loved."

As the pieces unfolded, it became clearer to me that this was evidence of the dark hating the light. Any opportunity to shame, dim, or cover my light was taken. That same supervisor made comments to the entire team *while I was on maternity leave.* "Hmm. She seems busy on leave. How do you have time to do all that she's doing if you're supposed to be on maternity leave?"

These were attempts to taint the water with my colleagues. There were countless examples of times I was shamed or scolded. Times that campus partners would request my presence at an event and she would tell me I needed to be more focused on getting my work done "instead of responding to outings" that were connected to our work. But again, I didn't understand what was happening at the time.

My favorite darkness-scattering interaction was a month after being in the office from maternity leave. Kristan texted me the night before our team building event around 9 PM to tell me to meet her, Becky Ivy (HRC), and Doug Welch (Kristan's boss, OGC) in HR. I told Gary, "They're going to try to fire me." He refused to believe it, but that meeting catapulted us into a crisis. A crisis we could have never anticipated when we said, "Yes, Lord. We'll follow your call."

In that meeting, they told me I had 30 days to do and make five pages of improvements. If I could not meet muster in those 30 days, it would be grounds for termination. They let me know that Kristan would be stepping out for the second part of our meeting. I assumed that this was the part of the meeting where I shared my perspective. Not exactly. This was the part of the meeting where they handed me a severance agreement. I could choose to do the impossible PIP, or I could sign the separation agreement, take my $40,000, and go on back to Virginia.

I was in total shock. I had no doubt in my mind I was called here. So much so that when I put in my resignation at Liberty, they offered to match what Baylor was going to pay me (over $85,000) and create the position I had proposed almost a year prior, which was an AVP-level position of Title IX, Civil Rights & Equity. I was making $58,000 as the Title IX coordinator at Liberty University—three direct reports and over eleven dotted line reports. I declined the position of my dreams, a significantly increased salary, keeping my family and friends close by, staying with what I knew, and having my baby where it was familiar because a beautifully wise and prayerful intern I had told me, "God leads. Satan follows."

Jesus was leading and Satan was following with counterfeits. I knew that, which was why Gary and I confidently said, "*Yes, Lord!* We'll go to Waco." So how did I end up here? Lord, this can't be you. How did you allow this to happen? The valley is dark. But here we were, in a valley.

But Jesus was still there and I knew He called us out here. So I quickly told them, "I'm going to do whatever I have to do in that PIP. I am a hard and committed worker. I'm going to get it done."

Doug Welch quickly retorted, "Even if you can, there are some other things we want you to do and if you can't do those things, that's grounds for termination as well!" I have to note, I had a really good idea of what those "other things" would be.

When I became the TIX coordinator at Liberty, I was the very first at this level and was given a team of investigators, which meant I had not done many investigations as an investigator. I disclosed this on my application, in my first interviews, and the interviews that followed. So, I had a very, very strong inkling to know that "the other things" were investigations of which I had very little "hands in the dirt" experience.

I was an administrator. Always had been. But they knew what they could align to set me up to fail. Even then, I did not understand how in four short weeks of work, my presence had merited such an aggressive exit party! Nonetheless, they told me not to talk to anyone outside of my family about this and I had a few days (that honestly felt like weeks). Some of the longest, most grueling days of my life. But still, God was with us in the valley. He faithfully and strategically sent words, visions, and people to strategically prepare for the throws of the warfare that we had found ourselves. We were *not* alone.

The weapons he provided to fight with were nothing short of divine, further solidifying that we had not made a mistake, and we were in the midst of a heated battle. He constantly reminded us that He was near. His presence was real. So real that in one of our lowest moments, the Lord spoke life and light into the dark through our Anastacia, who was three at the time.

We happened to be sitting at the food court of the Richland Mall in the days that followed this meeting, at this moment, Gary and I both were feeling particularly down. Neither had anything to encourage the other. We couldn't even look at each other. A moment of hopelessness. And without prompting, Anastacia stood up in her booth and said, "Praise the Lord." We both looked up. She repeated, "Praise the Lord!" And continued to repeat it until we joined her with the same level of enthusiasm! Breathing life into our broken hearts and bones.

Another example was the seemingly emotionally disconnected friend I mentioned previously, who sent me a text saying, "Hey. This verse came up as my verse of the day... I'm not sure what's going on, but I can't stop thinking of you—for what it's worth, 'Psalm 91:4, He will cover you with His feathers; you will take refuge under His wings. His faithfulness will be a protective shield.'"

So moments, interactions, and faithful people following the Lord's prompting spoke life into our bones. We listened intently for God's leading, prompting, and still quiet voice. And without fail, He used both the expected and unexpected to breathe life when we felt we didn't have the strength to inhale another breath. I am still in awe of how He consistently provided in those days—even prior to going into the first meeting.

Before that first meeting, as I lay in my bed before falling asleep, I heard the Lord quietly whisper, "When you get there, ask if you can open in prayer."

I calmly replied, "OK."

As I walked into the meeting with Becky, Doug, and Kristan, I sat down, and they jumped right in. I interrupted them and asked if they minded if I opened in prayer. I felt the roaches scrambling. I didn't see Doug's expression, but he didn't move. Becky quickly glanced at Kristan as if to ask if it was OK. Kristan scoffed and rolled her eyes.

Becky fumbled and said, "Oh! Uh... sure! OK. Uh, would you like to, uh, go ahead?"

And calmly and peacefully, I went to the Father, inviting Him into the space. The reaction to my ask was timeless. That was when what PJ told me started truly clicking. I was at a "Christian institution." But Christianity was a religion and a culture here. It was not a relationship where Jesus was genuinely a part of the fibers of who we are. Their Jesus sells tickets. Their Jesus keeps the stadiums full. Their Jesus keeps enrollment high.

Their Jesus keeps them rich. He doesn't convict. He doesn't encourage. He doesn't speak life.

I was beginning to realize that we were not serving the same god. As the years unfolded, I quickly found that walking with the Jesus I knew would come at a cost. A high one. A high one that most are not willing to pay…

We have debt but no regrets. We've been ostracized, but no regrets. We came to a foreign land but have no regrets. We said yes when people we trusted said we should say no, but have no regrets. Saying yes to the Lord, speaking truth to power, choosing to do what is right, and following your convictions, is always the bumpy, windy road less traveled. But it is a road marked with peace, promise, victory, and righteousness. A road where you will always feel fully alive because of how closely He, the life-giver, promises to walk with us. Yes, there will be difficulty, but no regrets.

***

The darkness sometimes reminds me of a swamp. There's growth that happens there, but oftentimes it smells, and it ain't pretty. Man-eating mosquitoes breed, and the water doesn't flow. A lot of these characteristics overlap with many of my impressions of human resources and the way that it has functioned in our nation. I know this because of the stories I hear from others on the job—corporate or not, higher ed or K-12, public or private—you name it, I've heard it.

I'm not sure what is taught in college in human resources, but one has to wonder if they cover sneakiness, manipulation, or bullying because of the handful of experiences that I've had with "Christian" human resources departments. Much of the staff operated ambiguously in those areas of specialty. That being said, that's why I feel the need to let that shit air, and

I am in a position to let that swamp breathe and get some water flowing through there.

For far too long, HR at Liberty and Baylor did all of their thriving in the shadows. Some of the slimiest behaviors I've ever encountered were in HR. They've mastered the art of bullying in a way that keeps them from being accountable to any entity or anyone. And it's time to change that narrative. I am primed to do that because I'm controlled by no one's HR but my own. There's clothes on my back and food on my table.

But let's be clear—it took courage and hard decisions to get here. And now, as an entrepreneur and consultant, I get to assist them in taking steps to operate with integrity and transparency by telling my truth for all to see and hear, and make decent money doing it! So you will unapologetically hear the numbers, the timing, the language, the titles, the threats, and the lies I've watched them (specifically Baylor) get tangled in for years. It's sad. But it's time for something different. After Jerry got exposed, it looks like they're doing a new thing at Liberty–unfortunately, it takes something like that to get there.

I would never go as far as to say that every individual who has a career or job in HR is a bully, but I will say that a lot of the "good people" are complicit and accessories before and after the harm is done by HR to humans. They've accepted a culture that they've been indoctrinated to accept. They have secret meetings, secret conversations, secret documents signed.

They say things like, "Hey, you can't tell anyone about what we talked about today, and if you do, that's grounds for..."

"You can't discuss with anyone what was decided today.."

"You can't share what you were offered today.."

"Sign here and agree not to say anything..."

There's no other way to describe it. Let's call it what it is and not manipulate it to be something we're more comfortable labeling it. It's sneakiness, and it's *bullying*. And it's done behind closed doors. As someone who had both dotted-line direct reports from HR and who the Lord strategically placed in the heart of the beast that is HR, I've seen it up close—and it ain't right. It's foul.

And it's time for a new thing.

Chapter 17: A Big 'Thank You'

We lost some dear "friends." I'm hesitant to use quotations, but can't bring myself not to. Perhaps a question mark best captures the heart of what I feel about said friends. To say we've been ghosted is an understatement. In some ways, it was to be expected. In other ways, a little more shocking.

As I mentioned, when we arrived on Waco rock, we were the *Neon Wardlaws*. Everywhere we went, we were seen. It felt like every casual conversation resulted in an effort to nurture a friendship. Whether it was a casual encounter at a farmers market that resulted in an invitation to dinner in someone's home that night or a tearful response to an altar call at church that yielded a monetary donation in our hands and an invitation to their life group. Or an unexpected conversation at an event that resulted in a dinner date and the purchase of our Waco home. These things were not random and sporadic. They were consistent and relentless.

Now, to give a little more context to our circumstances in 2017 and 2018, to say we were broke would be a mild understatement. Even though I had gotten a pay increase in my new job at Baylor, Gary had left his employment entirely to care for our children. Our beautiful first home in Virginia was still sitting on the market, waiting for its next family to call it home, all while we paid the mortgage. Our car notes were well above our means on one income. We were also paying for rent and then eventually a mortgage once we found our new home. A new home that we were extensively renovating and paying well above what we had been quoted by the "wanna-be-fixer-upper" contractors of Waco.

We were barely able to put Anastacia in pre-school but for two half-days a week. And quite frankly, we were fighting to put food on the table for some weeks, which was why we spent countless meals eating in the student dining halls. We were content nonetheless.

We chose joy whenever possible. But unless someone asked, they may have never known the extent of our financial deprivation. So it was nothing but divine intervention that we were regularly invited to peoples' homes to eat, that we could go to the altar to pray and come back to hundreds of dollars in our car seat. We had people in our lives who spent countless hours at our Waco home, using their trade, skills, and resources to complete the clinic and our house. We also had people give us thousands of dollars to finish our home without any expectation of repayment. It would be nothing for us to come home and find a package on our doorstep with goodies after having a baby—handmade baby clothes, towels, washcloths, and the like.

At first, we thought, *This is Waco*. But, we quickly realized that this was not typical. Not everyone feels as if people will recognize you everywhere you go and not hesitate to strike up a conversation—Target, H-E-B, Chick-fil-A, you name it, someone knew us.

God knew what we needed. We were halfway across the country, no family, and little to no financial resources. He provided and affirmed. You are right where you're supposed to be. And I am going to use the people around you to affirm that.

There were times when we desired to pay back or make it up to folks, but it was actually pretty impossible to do so. There really was no way we could if we tried. And as the season to speak up came and went, so did the "friends." But ironically, or as Most High would have it, the need was no longer there. As we were ushered into a new outspoken season, our finances had utterly turned around by this time as well. While 2020 left most people in one of the most difficult financial seasons they had ever seen, we found ourselves in one of the most prosperous seasons we had ever seen. While it was painful to have these "friends" suddenly disappear into the darkness, it was affirming and gratifying to see the faithfulness of God in our provision by means of our giftings.

After the dust settled and everyone was gone, while it was tempting to harden my heart and become callous to these "friends," I had to keep things in perspective. Many (if not most) were seasonal. However, many of them recognized the greatness in us and also felt compelled to be a part of sustaining and spurring us on. Unbeknownst to them, that call was leading us to a place many were not comfortable coming to, and they would eventually leave us feeling abandoned and betrayed.

But the proper perspective allows us to respond to those folks with nothing but a big "thank you." Thank you for being obedient—for feeding us, getting us in our home, for companionship, and support. Ultimately for what was a seasonal role in the fabric of our beautiful story of faith.

Chapter 18: The Road to Healing and Wholeness

"Type-casted"

It's like living in an invisible cage—one that I was taken by the hand and led into, and one I knew was there but didn't have the language or pessimism in my heart to see. It wasn't until I was sitting at a table at Panera Bread with a friend (also a former Baylor employee) that she casually stated one of the many reasons she decided to leave.

She said, "I had to realize that I was not getting promoted any time soon."

I asked, "How do you figure?"

She replied, "Oh, because we, as black people, get type-casted at Baylor."

And just like that, the cage where I functioned and did my best to thrive within for three and half years was illuminated. I ran through in my head the countless brilliant black individuals who fought and fought for promotions for years. Worked tirelessly, did work above and beyond the call of their roles, and yet remained in the same positions they were hired for.

Why was it that no matter how I performed, how much public praise I received, I was never a serious consideration for any position beyond the assistant project manager (of no one) role they had mitigated me to shortly after I returned from maternity leave?

The terribly conflicting reality in all of the aftermath of my departure is the countless black employees who are now receiving promotions and being highlighted and celebrated across news mediums. The terribly conflicting part is that, while I celebrate my brothers and sisters who are now getting the appreciation they deserve, I wrestle with the frustration in my heart of the reality that these individuals did not *all of a sudden* become incredible. It took incredibly threatening and eye-opening circumstances for the university to make decisions to intentionally put aside their typecasting ways and see the quality of black talent, skills, intelligence, and diligence right in their faces.

So, in the same breath, I celebrate my brothers and sisters and do my best to relinquish disdain for an institution that I believe is primarily driven and motivated by self-serving, public-facing interests.

The freedom that I now walk in outside of my type-casted cage may not be as sweet, as fresh, or as liberating had I not known what it meant to give everything I have and still be great while living in the confines of a box that was built and insulated to keep me contained.

Chapter 19: Grief Is a Funny Thing

Funny isn't exactly the word most of us would use for grief. It's simply the word to tritely reference its complexity. For centuries, psychologists, therapists, philosophers, and educators alike have tried to pin it down and explain its cycles, its implications, and the unpredictability in the human psyche.

Recently, God has given me a very clear revelation and insight about numerous things about my evolution of self. One of those insights was that it has always been incredibly easy for me to make sacrifices to advocate for everyone but myself. When it comes to myself, something in me didn't see the value in the same way.

Was I worth the time, energy, and resources it would take to speak up on my own behalf? Did something about it seem selfish? Did it not drive me as deeply as the injustices I witness on behalf of my family, friends, or even perfect strangers?

Nevertheless, while some of the questions still remain unanswered for me, there was a lot more clarity that had been made available. As much as I wanted to be able to move on with my life, spending time and energy cultivating the new passions and opportunities around me, there was a fight I had walked away from. In my pursuit of peace and normalcy and leaving behind a very painful chapter in hopes of a renewed chapter that involved lots of healing and forgetting, I failed to realize that there was still a story that needed to be told.

One of the most liberating aspects of walking away from Baylor University in the way that I did was that I got to talk about it without a muzzle. And "talking about it" was absolutely practicing what I preach. The freedom and healing that come from talking about your life's experience is necessary not only for your own ongoing recovery and grief but for the empowerment, liberation, and healing of others.

I have been reminded of this over and over again every time I get a DM about the journey that someone bravely embarked on that was inspired, motivated, or encouraged by my leaving that position.

What is heartbreaking for me at times is the belief that this position that I chose is for vain attention seeking, bitterness in the form of resentment for not having received a promotion, or ignoring my legal training or legal recourse to "properly handle the situation." We have many broken or seared relationships because of these warped perceptions of reality.

And what's even more heartbreaking is that in many of these relationships, I thought that they would have taken a very deep consideration of all that we sacrificed to speak up about what we and others were experiencing—even if we had not articulated at length what we had endured for years.

But grief is funny like that. I can go months without a thought of certain individuals or situations crossing my mind. And just like that, a smell, a song, a show, can trigger what one thought was forgotten. Time heals but doesn't always allow you to forget. I am grateful God's healing power continues to work in my heart and mind. But I am committed to be fully surrendered to Him as his vessel.

What that means for me is when He says, "It's time to speak up," when I have moved my family halfway across the country, I am the primary breadwinner and health benefits carrier, and I live in a town economically sustained by the institution I'm supported by, I'm going to do it.

When he says, "Walk away," when I am in the throes of negotiation with that said institution about my personal racial injustices at the height of the country's greatest racial unrest since the '60s, knowing that the implications of finishing this particular fight are financial instability for my family for the next few years (knowing we've known nothing but instability since we got here), I'm going to do it.

When he says, "Finish the book," even when I know the years and pain at Baylor are behind me—including friends and family who have since abandoned us, and I'll need to revisit things I hoped to have forgotten in order to fight injustice and speak truth on His chosen platform—I'm going to do it.

I am truly grateful for His patience and kindness and gentleness with me over the years. He was such a gentleman about my process. And He has graciously provided affirmations, when I was ready, to continue this journey of obedience. One thing that I've always been—and I blame my mother—is "tactful." I can't be sure of all the complexities of this said "tact" or decorum, but it greatly impacted my departure from Baylor.

I operated with this said tact, having had conversation after conversation behind closed doors advocating for marginalized people, hoping that my persuasive speech, work ethic, and personality would hold enough weight to make a difference. I operated with tact when I chose not to share with people how often I made project proposals and was dismissed, minimized, or scolded for doing so, only for those proposals to be given to a white female to be executed and praised.

I operated with tact when Gary and I secretly prayed, cried, and waited for me to be promoted into positions I drafted, proposed, and created—only for white women in power to identify the positions as failed searches or deceptively manipulate the process to keep me from getting a fair opportunity to be promoted.

I recognize why it's so difficult to believe or empathize with my story at times. Our tactfulness practices which are likely saturated in assimilation, kept me from providing the details of my daily life. Details that are so complex that I was often convinced that no one wanted to hear. One thing that did become painfully clear to me during weeks (what felt like countless months) of negotiations was that the more I laid out the timelines and the details of my experiences, the more validated I felt that this was much more than an emotional vengeance-seeking vendetta. This was a practice deeply rooted in this institution's DNA that had been nothing more than a rinse and repeat.

Unfortunately, most people were not in a financial position to do anything about their lived experience except cry about it, leave, and get paid to stay quiet. The body count of stories like mine is endless. I know I did not even begin to scratch the surface of what and to whom the institution had buried with unmarked graves. This is why the story has to be told, and the addendums and receipts are attached for your reference.

No more silent killings. No more private funerals. No more unmarked graves.

Chapter 20: The Plantation

I've often likened my experience to practices of slavery at Baylor. Even the simplest of parallels have always been astounding to me. Every position of leadership was held by white people. It was clear that there was a major shift in the gender of those white people after their very public Title IX crisis. But every position of leadership from the President's Council to the deans, and until recently, the chairs, have all been white people.

Is it reasonable to believe that the only qualified people for leadership were *white*? Given that the student population was approximately 30% non-white? And that Baylor University prided itself in recruiting both nationally and internationally for *the* most qualified individuals in many of their positions from faculty members, to directors, to coaches.

But the thing is, marginalization at this institution runs in its roots. Black people were not the only marginalized group, but in the years following the Title IX scandal, they had become one of the most organized and outspoken on the staff/faculty side, with LGBTQIA+ leading the pack on the student side.

***

Recently, Gary and I decided to watch "Harry & Meghan" on Netflix. It seemed interesting enough. We knew bits and pieces of their story—namely because of the work we do in racial equity. There are many events that happen where it seems like common sense to us, and we assume to others as well, that there is a swift racial undertow that's wiping out its victim unjustly. As little as we knew about Harry & Meghan's story, it seemed apparent, even from a distance, that any backlash, bullying, or hardship they were facing as this royal interracial couple was likely because Harry had the audacity to taint the pure white royal British line with some black blood. This "black blood" dates back centuries. For whatever reason, this "blood" was one that could change the course of history in an instant.

We enjoyed watching their love story. It reminded us so much of ours. It was beautiful and pure. An unlikely pair, but everything about them fit. They knew it. And they wanted others to know it as well as they did. Once married, they became very popular and quickly made a name for themselves around the world. They moved with such authenticity that people were drawn to their energy.

This "energy" radiated from both of them. But what was so inviting and stunning about Meghan's energy specifically was that she was new. She was a refreshing reset to the stale old, same old. Something that people around the world were yearning for.

But as we continued to watch their story unfold, something about it started to become chillingly familiar. She was winning the love, admiration, and attention of everyone near and far. She was quickly becoming the beloved poster child of the royal family. But this was clearly out of order and an abomination to the unspoken rules of order when it comes to hierarchy and elitism.

And unfortunately, whether she knew it or not, this will only be accepted for so long before there's a dark but calculated—concerted, but covert—effort to constrain, belittle, or denigrate her to her "rightful" or more appropriate position. Regardless of whether you worked for that place or, much more likely, have been elevated to that place by the people and community around you.

And that's where I deeply resonate with Meghan and the experiences she has had that seemed to parallel mine in time and space. I can't speak for her because I only know what I know from a documentary. But I can share exactly what I saw and experienced in my three-and-a-half years at Baylor University.

You see, Meghan mentioned over and over again that she wanted so badly to do exactly what they wanted and needed her to do. She wanted to be an asset to the family, not a distraction or a problem. She wanted to be accepted as one of them. She was willing to wear whatever helped her blend into the background (camel colors, tans, browns), and she learned the proper order of speaking and appropriate interactions. She worked to ensure that she was contributing above and beyond to the work of the Queen and the Commonwealth. But as much as she tried to do and say the right things and blend into the background so as not to compete with anyone, her light still shone.

Ironically, Baylor's tagline, "Where lights shine bright" is one that demonstrates in billboard fashion the hypocrisy of the institution. The expectation for lights to shine bright has limitations. It should come with very specific caveats and fine print of *whose* lights were supposed to shine bright. But you see, one of the lessons I learned with a front seat in the belly of the beast was that the marginalization of sexual assault victims was not a "bad hand that Baylor was dealt." It wasn't an unfortunate lot of circumstances that happened to land them on front page news. It actually is characteristic of the institution that is deeply embedded in the culture. Marginalization.

Unfortunately, for those out on the margins, you were a part of that fine print. Whether it was the marginalization of the LGBTQIA+ student or the marginalization of the Black staff member. There were most definitely exceptions for whose lights could shine bright. Until it's conveniently self-serving to the institution.

And that's what makes the stories of the marginalized few so difficult to tell. There are people all around you who are allowed and encouraged to shine bright. Unbeknownst to the world, you're doing everything in your power to shine appropriately, not too bright, not at the wrong time, in the wrong way, but on time in the way that makes them the most comfortable. But inevitably, you will misstep.

Your light will come out at the wrong place at the wrong time, and before you know it, all the work you've so tirelessly done to make sure you don't shine too brightly over those who are expected to shine is shattered in an instant. And you're left desperately trying to piece together and undo the "damage" that your light has caused.

All the while trying desperately to maintain your psychological stability. Because who can understand this dance you do from sunup to sundown? And any attempts to explain it are likely to leave you feeling exhausted and the listener skeptical, at best, but more likely critical, demeaning, and dismissive.

In hindsight, it's so painfully clear to see the dance I did. Day in and day out. My light was bright, which drew them to recruit and hire me. However, the expectation would be that I shine it "appropriately."

But when I stepped on that campus, the insecurity of the white women who supervised and managed me was aggressive and palpable.

Chapter 21: THE Performance Improvement Plan

I have heard *countless* stories with the same narrative. "I don't understand what happened."

"I had incredible performance evaluations year after year, and then all of sudden, I didn't."

"All of sudden, we're talking about a PIP. How did we get here?" The people and details adjusted slightly, but the narrative was always exactly the same and was followed by comments like, "I won't compromise my integrity."

"I had an idea that outshone an insecure supervisor."

"I present an idea, a concept, a project, and an initiative that challenges the status quo, and then all of a sudden, my performance is concerning, and we have questions of whether I'm a good fit for the institution or organization."

I had a new friend come over for brunch, a Black female who used to be at Baylor. As we sat and talked about all the great and miraculous things we'd witnessed the Lord doing in our journey, we couldn't help but note the kickback we received along the way. There seemed to be a theme—a pattern. It didn't matter the specific institution or organization, the pattern was the same.

As I listened to her share her corporate America story, it was no different than mine or the next intelligent, bold, hardworking, creative black woman. As I shared with her a little more of my Baylor story [from the letter to mediation to performance evals] she often finished my sentences. She said what was unique about me was that not many people have the grace, fortitude, poise, and integrity to walk away and be in a position to tell their story. She described it as a large ship that keeps moving but with a wake of black and brown bodies along the way.

I also recall a brown body that sat in my office. A faculty member who had been at the institution for years. Sharing story after story of the comments made along the way by colleagues, supervisors exposing their bias of this faculty member's race, and intellectual abilities. After being denied tenure, he met with Sallie and I several times to discuss his options. He pleaded, "What should I do?!"

We could see the turmoil and angst in his body. He was so vested but so stuck. As my colleague and I worked tirelessly for a form of recourse, we hit wall after wall and were told, "There's a process that has to be followed." And we all know full well that those processes were not created by us or for us, so at the end of the day, we always lose. So, eventually, we all had to accept the reality of being black and brown professionals at a PWI. Hence the endless wake of bodies.

As I've referenced time and time again, they did not come for my physical body as my ancestors have experienced, but they came for the emotional, psychological, and mental from day one. The legacy of our ancestors was to break us psychologically because of the strength that we bore. Strength that was apparent to those who desired to control us. So those in control don't dare to destroy us physically for a lot of obvious reasons—psychological defeat is the key to control.

Chapter 22: Violent White Women

Laura is one that I would have called a "friend" at the beginning of her tenure. She was hired by the institution as their Title IX coordinator in 2018—shortly after they declared the first AVP of equity position a failed search. As I mentioned, this was the same search that I submitted my application, and was only asked to fill out the first round questionnaire.

I remember completing it like it was yesterday. I remember so vividly because every question spoke to my soul. I was passionate, experienced, and deeply connected to every question and answer. I could not wait to participate in this process because I genuinely felt called to this position in every way.

This was the same search where the university had hired an outside firm to do the heavy lifting. Find the candidates for the pool, move those candidates through the process and land the university some strong options. By this time, it was late 2017, and I was starting to find my rhythm in HR. They told me that this position on my transition from under the workplace abuse of Kristan in Title IX was temporary until they could get the position off the ground that I had articulated to them, which was a position over equity.

So I was finding my groove in the meantime. I was creating where I had the opportunity—courses for employees to take to learn about bias and DEI, or even doing things like volunteering to write articles in the HR newsletter. So when HR made the announcement that they were doing a national search for the AVP of Equity, I didn't believe that this position was being afforded to nationally recruited candidates. I felt confident of my ability and experience to assume this role–even if it was up against candidates across the nation. No problem. But this wasn't a vain conceit. It was simply the confidence of call and anointing.

So it was no surprise to me that after I submitted my application, I happened to be working on a case that I wanted to chat with a professional mentor about. Scott had been one of my mentors for a few years at this point–since I had stepped into the Title IX role at Liberty back in 2014.

He and I met at a Title IX Conference where he was one of the primary partners and facilitators. I liked his energy and intellect. He was my 'go-to' whenever I was navigating complex issues and cases. So, on this particular day, early 2018, even though I hadn't talked to him since I left Liberty, I knew he was just a phone call away.

"Hey Britt! How are you holding up over there?!" he enthusiastically answered.

"I'm doing OK... it's been a little crazy."

He chuckled and replied, "I was literally just talking about you yesterday!" This surprised me a bit as we hadn't talked in awhile and Scott was actually a really big deal.

"Really?!" I replied, not really believing him and assuming he was just being flattering.

"Yeah!" And he proceeded to tell me that a search firm had given him a call and wanted him to make some recommendations. You see, this search firm was hired by Baylor University to find an AVP of Equity and needed some candidates.

"Yeah! I told the firm that they have a strong candidate right there at the institution!"

I was stunned. God, what are the chances? I knew what the Lord had for me was for me. But I never thought that with a JD, years of experience in Title IX, exposure to civil rights work right here at Baylor, passion, popular opinion, and the nomination of nationally recognized professionals in the field, Baylor still wouldn't give me a chance—not even to interview. Multiple times. The thought of putting an honest, passionate black professional into a position like that repulsed them so much that they elected to declare the search a failed one.

Now, while they were doing this search for the AVP of Equity, they were simultaneously doing the search for the Title IX position. By this time, Kristan and her toxicity had been effectively removed. The first year I was in HR, numerous professionals who were still reporting to her from Title IX would make their way to HR to sit in my office and cry, and I would take the opportunity to pray with, encourage, and empower them to go back to that toxic space. This happened weekly, if not daily.

Laura was the new Kristan. And even though the firm wouldn't give me a shot for the Equity position, they did ask the VP of HR if they could throw me in the Title IX Coordinator pool. How do I know? Well, the VP of HR was a chatty one. She would casually share things with me, clueless of the implications of her sharing. "I told him, oh no, we have other bigger and better plans for her!"

This naively fueled my hopefulness and expectation to do something in equity. She later shared that they hoped to hire a VP-level position of equity and put me directly under them. "With some mentorship, I think we can get you ready for a position like that." And I believed her. I believed everything she told me. I genuinely thought she cared. I mean, she was the one that "saved me from Kristan," so of course she cares about me. A misconception that proved fatal for my career at Baylor.

So when they hired Laura as the TIXC, I didn't initially have much interaction with her her first year because I was still in HR. But when the university created "The Equity Office" comprised of me and Sallie, and moved us back over to the Title IX space, I had a lot more opportunities to get to know her. She seemed nice and pretty down to earth. She was new to the area and was a new mom.

I was empathetic to the mommy of one and how challenging that adjustment can be as an executive-level professional. She and I talked about setting up playdates, I invited her to my home, and we had various meetings together throughout the work week. She leaned heavily on me and Sallie for civil rights/DEI-related advice and was always very affirming of the skillset we brought to the office. She was definitely a competent professional but was always honest and transparent about deferring to us when our worlds crossed.

So, needless to say, her disclosure as a final candidate in 2019 for the AVP of equity was a traumatic shock to my heart, mind, body, and spirit. But the writing was on the wall leading up to it. She and Driskell did seem to become very good friends very quickly. There was much about her that mirrored who Driskell was and, I'm sure, brought Driskell great comfort and familiarity as her supervisor. The familiarity that kept BIPOC perpetually in inferior positions—specifically at Baylor.

So once she announced that she was a final candidate for the position and also disclosed to her team that Baylor leadership approached her multiple times to apply after she initially showed no interest, it should have been easier to stomach when she was not only selected for the position but then simultaneously promoted to an associate vice president. Not only that, but she would be one of my new supervisors, bumping me down two levels further below Driskell.

I very quickly decided that I wanted to be very forthright with Laura in this new relationship dynamic. I was not sure at this point the impression that Driskell had given her of me, but I didn't want to leave any room for something ugly to fester and cause any issues in our working relationship. So, one afternoon after it had been announced, but before she assumed the role, I decided to ask her if she and I could meet. She agreed.

I think I spent roughly 30 minutes to an hour in her office, doing my best to humbly communicate my heart and perspective. I wanted her to know that I had applied for the position and that I had been very interested for some time.

"I am hurt about the way things played out, but I need you to hear from me that I am still very committed to doing the work of this office and supporting my leadership in the process." She apologized with what seemed like genuine (or perhaps mustered up) empathy for the way things went and listened intently but also typed feverishly to transcribe our entire meeting. One can only conjecture what the nature of her motives was at this time.

But, my goal in this communication was to be forthright and authentic so as not to leave any room for a twisted counter-narrative of my heart or perspective about the university's decision—as devastating as it was to me.

I left her office feeling free and very much at peace. I definitely left with a confidence that I had done my due diligence to keep Driskell from tainting or maligning me to my new supervisor in any way.

The peace was undeniable. But perhaps, I left too confident. In the months that followed, it became clear to me that my efforts were in vain. It's not clear to me how or where the shift was happening. I have vague recollections of one or two interactions that weren't the friendly, peaceful engagements we once had. To say the relationship soured, I believe, would be a gross overstatement. But I'd be lying if I said it didn't change. The change in the air was palpable.

Could it have been me? Were the accolades for her and her lack of experience getting to me? Was the ease for which she was hoisted into this position vexing my soul? Was the bewilderment of her being given my project(s) and told to run with them, giving me ulcers? Was the mental and psychological defeat of working tirelessly for a position you were passionate about causing my smiles to break down? Perhaps.

The mental anguish and emotional management may have tipped the scales on my bubbly and professional interactions for the worse. I may have finally begun to unravel. The extra mile we have to run, the more tax we have to pay, and the more fancy dancing we have to do to prove we are worthy, capable, or competent had finally bankrupted my soul. It's the only reasonable explanation I now have for my near unraveling in our final interaction—my performance review meeting, virtually, April 2020.

A meeting that is forever seared on my mind and heart. A meeting where I had to listen to her tell me that she and others have found me "difficult to work with, my morale is too low, and I create obstacles." Feedback that she claimed stretched "*faaaaaar* beyond her, Robyn, and HR." Even listening to that recorded conversation is demoralizing.

I clearly recall in that moment I was composed and broken all at the same time. I was fighting a losing battle in a dark room with no protection or weapons. I had to sit and listen to this violent white women, heavily armed by other violent white women that she knew she had in her corner, and yet fight to maintain my composure at all cost. Because anything I said, or did in that meeting would absolutely be used against me to finalize my professional demise.

For every BIPOC or marginalized individual who has had to sit and endure circumstances that you know were manipulated against you to keep you on the fringes or push you out of the ring, know that I see you, I hear you, I empathize with you, and you are not alone.

It feels lonely and psychologically debilitating, but as our beloved, late Maya Angelou[22] reminds us, "still I rise."

...

You may write me down in history
with your bitter, twisted lies,
you may tread me in the very dirt
but still, like dust, I'll rise.

Does my sassiness upset you?
Why are you best with gloom?
Cause I walk like I've got oil wells
pumping in my living room.

...

Did you want to see me broken?
Bowed head and lowered eyes?
Shoulders falling down like teardrops.
Weakened by my soulful cries.

Does my haughtiness offend you?
Don't you take it awful hard
'Cause I laugh like I've got gold mines
Diggin' in my own backyard.

...

You may shoot me with your words,
You may cut me with your eyes,
You may kill me with your hatefulness,
but still, like air, I'll rise.

Chapter 23: The Casualties

"Let's be clear about what is actually at stake here... it's like symbolic annihilation. If you can destroy people who are symbols of social justice, then you can scare people to not want to go public. It is a way to signal to the rest of us to stand down." – Meghan Markle

"As sad as it is, in order for change to happen, sometimes a lot of pain has to come to the surface. In order for us to be able to move to the next chapter, we have to finish the first chapter." – Prince Harry, Duke of Sussex

***

The emotions of being a casualty are sometimes unspeakable. You explore the range of rage, defeat, bewilderment, abandonment, disbelief, loss, helplessness, and invisibility. But in the midst of all of these very real and very big emotions lie triumph. To be a living casualty is unlike anything you can tangibly touch. Because it's the spirit that lives on.

Yes, a part of you died, but an even bigger part of you lived—lived to see what has come to fruition on the other side of your death. Many who suffer physical death never get to know how deeply and widely their death has impacted today. But they also are spared the agony of watching what grows on their grave.

As I look at Baylor University, I can't help but wonder what flowers, trees, and grass are flourishing on top of the professional and psychological graves of so many who died fighting and trying to get the university to live up to its ideals. I now watch from afar as many of my suffocated, abused, and aborted visions and passion projects that held my heart and soul are truly being birthed into something beautiful.

The human emotion of feeling like a casualty is real and undeniable. It is one that I have to face, acknowledge and accept. I don't get to be on the highlight reel of what has come to fruition. I don't get to be acknowledged as someone who helped Baylor become who I hope that they are authentically leaning into.

Me and many, many others with unmarked graves are left to admire the flowers from afar, choosing to believe that our personal sacrifices were not in vain, choosing to believe that Baylor has and will continue to evolve past the prioritizing appearances of its image and reputation, above the livelihood of countless black and brown individuals and their allies.

Hearing about the marker for the 'unknown enslaved,' I truly cannot help but empathize deeply with my ancestors who left their blood, sweat, and tears on that campus—building it into what it is now. They died for that institution. Without them, the institution wouldn't be what it is. But we'll never know their names.

Am I envious of them? To say yes, would hardly be mildly insensitive, recognizing the egregiousness of what they endured in their lifetime. But it does beg the question—Is it better to have died having sacrificed so much for the institution and never knowing what it built on top of your grave as an unknown? Or is it better to watch from afar, having lost so much at its hands, and watch it build on you as an unknown?

These are questions that myself and many others may have to wrestle with. Notwithstanding the fact that many of the living casualties have received some form of reparations. For many, it was at the expense of their silence—forever and always muzzled from walking in the freedom and liberation of telling their story.

Nevertheless, may my ancestors rest in peace—unaware of what was built at the expense of their lives.

Chapter 24: What It Feels Like to Try So Hard and It's Still Not Good Enough

As much as I thought that my high school and childhood relationships were just something to briefly look back on and think of how much of a child I truly was fifteen to twenty years ago, it's amazing how many life lessons I learned in such a short but critical developmental time.

People often ask, "What was before Gary? Was there a 'before Gary?'" And there was—for most of college, in fact. I learned many lessons about myself—who I am, who I want to be, and who I was becoming.

I had a boyfriend who we'll call Tavion. He and I had been together off and on for over five years. Our last go at it, I really thought we had matured enough to take steps toward marriage. By this time, I was in my second year of law school and was learning to find my voice in a way that I had not before. Many (if not most) of the most pivotal turning points in my life have involved me finding my voice in a new way. Law school demanded it. I speak up to defend myself or get eaten alive. I had to find the belief in myself deep down. Without it, the environment smelled the weakness and vulnerability and sought to break you in many ways. This experience was multifaceted because one felt it academically and professionally, psychologically and emotionally, as well as socially and relationally. It was truly, survival of the fittest.

Needless to say, I was changing. So by the time he and I got back together, I was not quite as timid or wayward. I could hold my own space just a little bit better. It was obvious that this evolution made him a bit uncomfortable, but we trudged through it as best as any emotionally immature 22 or 23-year-olds could. We had been long distance for most of our relationship so I decided I needed to take a trip to visit him. Unbeknownst to the parents, I decided to use one of my academic breaks to spend time with bae. I felt if we were serious about this, we needed to share space.

I booked a flight and headed south. Overall, it was a good trip. Seemingly no glaring deal breakers. We spent most of the time engaging in activities I really enjoyed. Sightseeing around the city. Visiting civil rights landmarks and museums. And breaking bread with the occasional packed lunch in a park or by a pond. He even wined and dined me for *his* birthday at the very fancy and luxurious Cheesecake Factory. Needless to say, it was a trip full of fun—for me.

He had made arrangements for me to stay at the La Quinta. Not my first choice. But he wasn't comfortable with me staying at his house—for reasons I suspect were related to cleanliness or the home life of the family. He wasn't a big talker, so I'm not too sure. Nevertheless, he and I stayed at this hotel. Even though I wasn't thrilled about it, I understood that I was staying longer than just a few days, and multiple nights in a hotel for a new college graduate working entry-level retail was quite a financial burden.

Like I said, overall, the trip was good. No major hiccups, and we had a full, fun schedule, which is on par with how I like to function. I flew back to Lynchburg to hop back into the semester feeling–so so. I was picked up from the airport by one of my roommates and dear friends, Murna. She let me know she would be going to grab some food with one of her friends from her job and asked if I was OK with joining. "Love to!" We made our way to IHOP for some chatter and debriefing over pancakes.

"I mean, it was cool," I replied as her friend asked all the questions to get the "T" on my semi-secret getaway.

"Just cool?!"

"I mean, it was really sweet... he took me to museums and out to eat, and we had meals in the park... I mean, he was really trying..."

"OK? What's the problem?" And with a tiny bit of hesitation, I blurted out, "He put me in the La Quinta! The one that has the doors to the outside!" Laughter erupted. I think partially because of how emphatic I was about my disapproval, but I think also because Murna knew me and knew that Tavion had missed the mark.

I tried to clean up my disapproval of my lodging by insisting on how much Tavion really tried during my stay to do all the things that made me happy. "He was really trying though y'all... I appreciate his efforts!" And with that, I heard a slow groan from her friend that I will never forget.

I looked at him, and he slowly shook his head and very matter-of-factly stated, "This ain't never gon' work."

"What do you mean?" I shot back.

He paused and said, "There's nothing worse than a man giving his best, and it still isn't good enough..."

My stomach dropped. I didn't say it at the time, but deep inside, I knew he was absolutely right. When you give your best efforts to anything, and it's not good enough, there's no salvaging the relationship. That relationship is, and will always be, on life support. Needless to say, hearing that truth could not be unheard for me—the bell couldn't be unrung. That relationship that I thought was my forever was over within a month.

I spent those years at Baylor trying to create, inspire, envision, cultivate, and impress anyone who had any authority to notice me and have any influence on my professional status. After taking the initiative to be a member of a steering committee to start Baylor's first ERG, I followed it up with a book club with executive administrators to inspire and enlighten their anti-racism efforts across campus.

I continued to move in my anointing to diffuse a national, news-worthy dispute between the student Texas Conservatives and the LGBTQ community, as well as implement and mobilize an online educational course for the entire campus in less than three months. I was then nominated by a national voice in Title IX & Equity as a strong candidate for a national search—and yet, I still did not get an interview for a promotion that I was qualified for. More on these efforts later.

The reality that my best efforts would never be good enough was beginning to ring deep inside. This relationship was on life support. And eventually, someone had to make the decision to pull the plug.

Part 5:
Runteldat Way

June 2020

Chapter 25: Baylor as the Gold Standard

One of the greatest appeals about responding to being wooed by Baylor throughout my initial interview process and into my executive third-round interviews was this notion that Baylor had the ability, the capital, and (seemingly) the desire to be the gold standard in a lot of ways in the world of scholarly Christian higher education. The world watched from afar as Baylor cleaned up all of its very messy defecation around Title IX and sexual violence in a very public way. Trying to salvage and rebuild their reputation as a reputable Christian institution.

I was familiar with the gravity of the investigations that were ongoing because as the Title IX Coordinator at Liberty, I was entrenched in the field. Baylor was undergoing all of the worst case scenario scrutiny that every practitioner in our field fasted and prayed to avoid at all cost. But to most of us (if not all), these looming and impending investigations felt inevitable. It was not a question of if, but when.

Would it be the Office of Civil Rights? Would it be a lawsuit from a disgruntled and expelled respondent or a scorned and tattered complainant? Maybe the NCAA or your collegiate conference? Always looking over your shoulder or around the corner. They were like boogiemen. Which is why we all watched in horror as the boogie man showed up at every door and window at Baylor University. Of course, hindsight is 20/20.

When Baylor responded with what seemed like transparency and authenticity, I thought, *Wow, what a refreshing change of pace from the southern Christian university I was at.*

I recall being in my boss' office at Liberty at the time, discussing Baylor's response to getting caught with their pants down and ass out, but this was around the same time I was in the interview process with Baylor. I vividly remember him saying to me, not knowing I was potentially on my way there...

"It seems like they're doing a lot of scapegoating to me, don't you think?" I also remember feeling deeply offended. *How dare he accuse their bold steps to right their wrongs in such a transparent and courageous way, scapegoating?* I pondered to myself.

"No, I don't think so," I naively and confidently replied. Why do any of this so publicly unless you want the world to keep you accountable, right? Or, as I would eventually discover, you have paid a lot of money to have a publicist company be very strategic about what will make you appear as above board as possible—sacrificing anything and everything to restore your image and brand—with or without integrity.

As the story goes, I found myself in BU Human Resources as one of two employees overseeing EEO for the institution. I was excited and hopeful about the role because of what I was verbally told by the VP of HR and her highest minion Becky—the Director of HR Consultants.

"Is there anything else you would want to do here at Baylor?" As they sought to find me a new position in the institution to ensure that there were no more waves caused anywhere near Title IX.

"Yes, there is, actually," I replied. "I would like a position to oversee equity. You don't have anything like this... and I drafted and was offered this same position while I was at Liberty." The VP went on to explain how she had met with the CFO that morning, Reagan Ramsower and discussed and received approval for that very position. She expressed her excitement about my interest, communicated that Becky would need a few days to get it drafted and situated, and that they would get me all set up in a week or so in the role.

By the time I came back, they had given me a temporary office space in HR, until they made space for me elsewhere. A space that was inevitably a large closet with no windows. Nonetheless, I was excited, hopeful, and relieved. I was exiting the stress, turmoil, and bullying in Title IX, and I was vested in this new hopeful opportunity in what was supposed to be the role of my dreams.

It's likely that my hopefulness for the best blinded me from the reality of the landfill I was actually working in, but I was motivated nonetheless. Still believing that I had arrived at an institution that wanted to do what was right because it was right. One that now knew better and wanted to do better. So even when they gave me a job description that assisted a manager who supervised no one, who reported to a director deeply embedded in HR, I was still believing and hoping for the best.

And what drove my hope was the faulty belief that Baylor's primary motivation for spending millions on hiring Title IX Office staff, paying for external investigators, paying for expert panelists, paying for external consultations, increased professional development budgets, updated office suites, was because they were invested in doing what's right and caring for the marginalized well.

The sad reality was that they were invested in saving the brand—at any cost and at the expense of anyone. Saving me was not from a place of goodwill—it was primarily from a place of saving the brand. So, while I thought overseeing the rest of the marginalized population would mean I, too, would see the same energy, resources, and enthusiasm to back my efforts, I would soon find out that could not be further from the truth.

There was no real scandal or cause for concern with other marginalized groups. Therefore, there was no real reason to allocate resources, time, or energy there either—until they had to...

Chapter 26: The Big Wins That Meant Nothing

Do you know what it feels like to be "in the pocket?" What do I mean by that? I mean, anytime you get in a space where your creativity is flowing, or you feel like you're operating in the fullness of you. It's knowing that whatever you're creating is really, really good. It doesn't *really* matter who else agrees. Regardless of the response, deep inside, you know it's good. It's nice to be affirmed, but it's not truly necessary.

I had a few mile-marker moments like that during my time at Baylor—what should have been good career-defining moments. But because of how I had been "typecasted," they were neutralized in my Baylor career trajectory. What's interesting, though, is that in my final hours (not literal hours, but the final defining interactions), some of the feedback I was given on my last evaluation was that I "lacked initiative and vision."

They inferred that they needed someone who was going to be a visionary for the work of equity at Baylor. And ironically, in most of the mile-marking moments I've referred to, I was scolded, questioned, or minimally acknowledged by my supervisor(s) for the work I was doing. Nevertheless, when engaging in these projects and the work across campus, my colleagues enthusiastically communicated their unwavering excitement, appreciation, and support.

"Britt, this was incredibly eye-opening!"

"Thank you for doing this—I didn't think we could pull this off."

"How were you able to execute this so quickly?"

"Where'd you come up with this idea?!"

These are the moments that I kept the painful dismissals to myself.

One project, in particular, was born from a place of need. I'd even go as far as to say desperation. There were two areas that Baylor often found themselves in the spotlight—if it wasn't Title IX, it was around their response to the LGBTQIA+ community at the institution. For those of us that worked in mid- to upper-administration, we were well aware that student groups received sponsorship and funding through the *Student Government Association*. However, the LGBTQ group on campus was allowed to meet but denied funding per the directive of the Board of Regents. This often created a lot of tension around the topic. So typically, no one wanted to have to navigate the politics associated with this group.

Unfortunately, this became unavoidable after an explosive interaction ensued between the group and the student-led Young Conservatives on campus—ultimately making national news. As days went on, more interactions ensued as tensions continued to rise around both Baylor's response and the students' public discourse with one another. All I remember about it was that it was very contentious, and the public was watching. And we all held our breath to see how Baylor would respond.

I didn't think much of it because I knew that situations like these rarely involved Sallie and me (even though we were in the Equity Office—a pretty good indicator that we weren't *actually* a legitimate facet of the university).

I received a call from a colleague I would soon consider a friend back then–he was the director of all things student activities. He reported to the VP of Student Life, who was also a big fan of mine. And I know because the VP would "secretly" call me from his cell phone to get my opinion and advice about equity matters. Why? Because he needed to bypass Driskell, and calling me on my personal cell was the only way to do that.

It felt like some real evil stepmother stuff where she's got the daughter who's actually wanted and kept her locked in the tower. Sure, we were allowed out of our Clifton Robinson Tower—but not to interact with anyone on her level unless she supervised the interaction. Driskell would go to great lengths to keep that from happening.

So the director that called, had an idea and he needed my help. He shared with me that he knew how experienced and versed I was in the work of Restorative Justice, and he was navigating a minefield with the Young Conservative and LGBTQ student groups that were making national news. His idea was that he and I work together to facilitate a *Restorative Circle*.[23]

Now, I could tell he was slightly hopeful but much more nervous about this venture. Likely because if this went south, potentially his career trajectory could, too. Or, perhaps, he had nothing to lose and everything to gain. Either way, it was a big risk and it appeared he felt strongly that he couldn't pull it off alone.

I can't say with confidence that I understood the risk we were taking, but just like any project that I went out on a limb at Baylor, the Lord covered me and breathed life into anything I touched. I won't bore you with the details of the long process of preparing this group. The people and hours it required to ensure every individual that was participating was vetted and well prepared for this Restorative Circle. I even spent several hours consulting with the trainers that Laura had flown out that summer to facilitate the training where the director had learned of my previous experience and skills in the work.

The consultant repeatedly said to me, "Britt, I think this may be a lose-lose situation for you. In the likely event that these groups don't go well, you'll be scapegoated for this. And in the unlikely event that they do go well, you may be tokenized." He had done this work for over twenty-five years and he was very trepid about the success of these sessions. He sent repeated warnings to which I peacefully and confidently replied, "It can be done."

I'll never be able to articulate the peace I felt about this whole project. Again, I was in the pocket. And all the peace and confidence I felt about the endeavor manifested in a miraculously fruitful circle! There were tears, there was laughter, there was peace and reconciliation! It was more than the director and I could have ever imagined it would be. There were no words to explain the miracle he and I were a part of! And we were over the moon.

The days that followed, my heart was full. I shared with Gary my shock and enthusiasm about the outcome and tried to recapture the power of the details and energy and flow in the room. All the while he looked with that beautiful, bright eyed, but oh so peaceful stare he gives me. And every time he says with his eyes, "I never doubted you. I know I'm married to greatness. I just wish you knew, too."

The days that followed should have been no surprise to me. There was radio silence from anyone on my end. But I don't think I expected to receive anything. Most of the time, when I successfully operated in these spaces, I was either scolded or ignored. So, the quiet days after the fact were par for the course. I wish I could say I was unaffected by the email exchange that followed, but if that was the case, you wouldn't be hearing about it right now!

"*Great job, Matt and Brittney! You guys did a wonderful job coordinating and facilitating an incredible opportunity for our students! We are so grateful for all of the extra time and energy you put into making this happen. We appreciate your strong leadership in moving us forward.*" – Kevin, VP of HR

Reply all:

"Matt, thank you for such a productive meeting and your leadership on this." – Robyn, Chief of Staff

Yep, you read that right. And just like that, Driskell ignored me, refused to acknowledge my contributions, and subtly—but in a very calculated manner—reminded me of my place.

And those were the moments that were ingrained; the wounds that flare up when I'm told in my performance evaluation that I lack vision or initiative; the subtle moments intended to break me down.

***

Creativity is truly a representation of the Creator. The way that He spoke and breathed life into all that is into being is undeniably creative. I was recently a keynote at a Women's Conference, and as I prepared for this time with these ladies on Proverbs 31 (one of my favorite passages), I was reminded how she "works with eager hands." (v.13). When we are in a space of creating, it's easier to work with "eagerness" or enthusiasm. I found spaces like these wherever God has placed me—whether at Liberty University, Baylor University, The Relationship Clinic, or BW Consulting.

Those opportunities were constantly arising, in spite of the backlash that I would endure. One instance, in particular, is probably one of my greatest contributions in my efforts to encourage a shift in anti-racist practices at Baylor.

Dr. Jemar Tisby had just released a book entitled, *The Color of Compromise*. This book was a brilliant articulation of the history of racism in American Christianity and the Church–providing a historical survey, noting the pattern of silence *and* outright contribution of racist practices by the White Evangelicals.

The idea to facilitate a book club at Baylor struck me without question. It seemed obvious, doable, and needed! I quickly formulated a plan, ironing out all of the administrative details. I would invite administrators that I had formed relationships with—individuals that were primed for the conversation, potential allies that had significant influence in their areas of oversight.

I thought, *If I can get them to go, it will trickle down and have an undeniable impact on the university at large"* And I was right. The foresight to know and understand who the best individuals to invite was a work that I can give credit to no one but the Spirit. Participants included provosts, general counsel, tenured professors, and deans. There was insightful dialogue, human connection and reckoning, and tears.

No one came to that group and left the same. It ran somewhere between six and eight weeks. The few sessions that were missed by any individuals were prefaced with an email expressing deep regret that something on their calendar was immovable in spite of their best efforts.

My relationship with these individuals was real, impactful, and deep. I could have never anticipated how powerful this time would be for us relationally and the unfettered commitment that all of these individuals had to be there every week. I believe the influence that time had on every human heart was something that I believe outlived my career at Baylor. I wish I could say that the creativity, initiative, and administrative organization that it required to pull that off and pull it off well was something that boosted my career trajectory.

But as one perceives the thematic patterns of my experiences at Baylor, it was predictably minimized and dismissed. Even though my supervisor had given me permission to do a book club, it was clear she was aggravated by the feedback and enthusiasm she had to listen to on a daily basis in her administrative "C-Suite" offices.

An unlikely provost participated in the group that was excited about our new bond, emphatically expressing to her, "I'm her [Brittney's] favorite!"

To which she irritably replied, "It's not that serious."

Driskell even managed to find a way to reprimand me for the work done with this group. I don't think she knew that when I requested approval for this project that I would have so many influencers in the group. "Next time you do something like this, I want to see the list of invitees and give approval first. These people are very busy and have other priorities. Their schedules don't need to be bogged down," she said.

In other words, *I didn't know you had the ability to connect and influence this professional level, and I don't like it. And I don't plan to let this happen again.* All the while... my performance evaluation reflected that I lacked initiative and vision...

***

In August 2020, one month after my resignation, Baylor announced that they would be mandating an online equity training for every member of the Baylor community—staff, students, faculty.

Approximately one year prior to that, Driskell declared that the President wanted the Equity Office to create and launch this training before the end of the year, 2019.

Now, having come from an institution where we had already undertaken this feat, I was pretty familiar with the process. I understood the logistics of timelines involved, the staff member expertise needed, and the administrative buy-in required. This was no three-month project. But, I also knew if I could leverage my professional relationships, put my work ethic and administrative skills into high gear, and draw from my experience, this would be something that Driskell could not deny as a noteworthy professional accomplishment!

And as the Spirit would have it, and to my disbelief, everything fell into place. I formulated a team with high-level marketing and public relations professionals. I worked with everyone from IT (Information Technology) to the Student Success Center. A project like this usually takes at least a full academic year due to the elaborate number of moving pieces that have to align with the timelines of the academic year.

I met with the team for weekly check-ins and assigned various tasks required to move things along quickly. And within three short months, to everyone's disbelief, we were ready to launch!

Along the way, I had given Driskell ongoing updates. She actually seemed very pleased with the progress. For the first time during our working relationship, it felt peaceful, cordial, and somewhat natural. I was thrilled. The week of the launch, everyone was crossing T's and dotting I's, and I would have one more brief interaction with Driskell before go-time. She had recently had a meeting with the President's Council and provided updates before the launch. Shortly after the meeting, she alerted me that we needed to talk.

And just like that, she was pulling the plug.

"Wait... what's happening?" I dumbfoundedly queried.

"They just had some questions about the content," she casually said.

"So why didn't you just share the content with them, Robyn?"

And with the same simple, blank, and clueless stare she gave when her critical thinking skills had carried her as far as they could, she mumbled something like, "Oh... I don't know." And that was the end of it. Nothing in her felt compelled to advocate for her direct report, who spent countless hours to pull this off. Nothing in her felt the need to acknowledge or even empathize with all the work I had put in to make this happen.

And just like that, I was left to pick up the professional ruble of my heart. Shattered in the street without even the decency to come sweep it up. And just like that, I picked up my pieces and went back to my temporary team and the countless campus partners I rallied.

I told them, as graciously as I could, how much I appreciated them and was so thankful for their participation and engagement to pull off the impossible. "We couldn't have done it without you."

A few were surprised. A few were in utter disbelief. But no one was more devastated than me.

But I'm not sure when I felt more devastation—when they pulled the plug or when they launched once I was out.

Chapter 27: "The Budget"

To say my family left Waco is arguably both overstated and understated. Wherever Gary and I go, we make it home. We invest ourselves, our family, our vision, our finances, our efforts into a space. We had made Waco home in more ways than one. So if one were to say we left, it's only because it had become very clear that it was no longer home. Waco once made space for the Wardlaws.

Where one once had great influence, when you speak truth to power, that space can vanish or shrink very, very quickly. So did we leave? I would argue that Waco left us in 2020. But even though we purchased our new primary residence in Dallas in 2021, we have been in Waco almost every week—working, socializing, and investing in the community. We always felt called here. We saw the brokenness in a lot of ways and have always been committed to being a part of the city's healing process. But the quirky thing about Waco is that they have to *allow* you into that process, and where we've been allowed or invited at this point has been very limited due to the shrinking process.

Nevertheless, we have persevered. Week after week, I-35 South, I-35 North, one hour, seventeen minutes without traffic. Our family knows this drive well. And with this drive, week after week, I often get a little chuckle about the (unprompted) commentary of my four children about Baylor University, which has grown, expanded, and developed beautifully right off the highway–with great intention, I'm sure. The institution's presence is undeniable off this main interstate that runs through the entire State of Texas, north to south.

At one point in time, it was difficult to drive past Baylor unaffected–particularly the Clifton Robinson Tower, due to all of the painful associations and grief of unmet expectations. However, I am so thankful for this drive now because I can see how far I've come in my healing journey. This view is a reflective look at my scars rather than a painful look at my wounds.

We have driven up and down I-35 and have made casual observations of how things have been constructed and developed—expecting no less from a growing institution and city. But one construction project in particular really got me thinking and reflecting—reliving very significant moments in my time at the institution. For months, I thought the new basketball stadium was actually a parking garage! Did that make sense? Probably not. But to be quite honest, I didn't spend enough time trying to figure it out.

Having to stay in Waco often in a hotel, we spent a great deal of time (and money) eating out. Some of our usual places would get old, so we started exploring some new ones. One evening we found ourselves at a restaurant we had seen but never visited, right across the river from Clifton Robinson—my old office, next to where the "parking garage" was being built. Per our norm, we made conversation with our server (or she made conversation with us). She told us a little bit about herself and when and how she started working here at this particular restaurant.

She was a young black woman, a single mom who had been a server at another local restaurant for years. She said she had a cousin convince her to try working here. She went on to share, "The owners are going to be doing quite a bit here soon… they're going to have more eating spaces downstairs on the water so that when the stadium's finished, donors and alumni can take a boat across to come eat…"

Ahh. A stadium. They were building a basketball stadium. Now, when we were a part of the Baylor/Waco community, you would have thought we were legacies of the institution, born and bred—we were all in at every game and sport possible. *Invested.* The Wardlaws were regulars at the basketball stadium, whether it was for a men or women's game or an acrobat & tumbling tournament, we were stadium frequenters.

Having been regulars at the stadium, I can tell you with confidence that with the regular gamegoer's eye, that stadium was great. There's very little in me that says it was due for reconstruction. But, hey, when there's a "budget" for it, anything can be due for a reconstruction, I suppose?

But the construction of this stadium definitely got me thinking and reflecting on how many times I was told there was no money in "the budget" for my equity-related project proposals. One project, in particular, was something I birthed while on maternity leave with my *Mercy* girl. Some of my best ideas and creative expressions come while I'm in my fourth trimester. I had been thinking at length about both the Title IX and equity work and how we could, as an office and institution, do it better.

One of the most painful intersections of the work was investigatory outcomes. For anyone who has done this work for more than a day, it's difficult to feel like and believe at the end of an investigation that anyone has "won." No party truly leaves feeling whole—even when there is a finding of responsibility. So as I reflected on the work and the processes that we had created in both offices, it hit me—I needed to use my skills and experience with restorative justice and mediation to build out the alternative resolution element of the offices. It was something we referenced in the policies as a potential option for participants, but because there was no real structure in place, it was rarely an option that was actually utilized.

So I spent time during my months of leave chewing on this and working it out in the form of a job proposal. At this point, it was clear that the

Equity Office and its leadership lacked vision. I had ideas for days because I was passionate about the work. Any idea I had, I would spend time thinking, praying and talking to my colleague about how to propose it to Driskell on the path of least resistance.

How could I couch it in a way that she didn't feel intimidated. Nothing about her was an advocate–not for us and not for this work. So when I brought ideas they had to be full proof because she was not in the business of doing anything that didn't make her look good or cause her to go against the grain in any way.

So, when I came back from leave, my angle was easy. The alternate resolution was an opportunity to have less angry people—everybody wins. Needless to say, she loved it. I'm not sure I can remember another occasion where she showed more enthusiasm. I was elated. This was an opportunity for me to move into more of a forward-thinking, visionary-building leadership role. I may not be leading the charge of equity, but I could heavily influence the culture of the work at the institution at large.

This was January 2019, and by this point, I had already put my hat in for the institution's first attempt to find an AVP of equity in January 2018. In spite of not being invited past the first screening questionnaire, I was not about to let that rejection stop me from continuing to pursue work I felt called to do. So this job proposal was a director or AVP level position.

It allowed me to create and build for both the Title IX and Equity Offices and truly transform the culture of a major sticking point at the institution. And, having done extensive alternative resolution work at Liberty, *for years*, not only as an overseer, but as a creator in expanding the vision for a very similar institution, I had the experience to back me.

A couple of the staff members in the office at the time knew the experience I had with the work and they were also curious and motivated about expanding in this area for our office for the good of their students that they had seen broken by the system as it was. They had begun to read material and look for conferences to learn more about alternative resolutions.

This was my baby at Liberty, so I was always happy to talk with them at length about the concepts and how we'd seen it play out, and especially how powerful the outcomes were for the institution–particularly the students. So, I knew it wouldn't be too difficult to rally the team around the concept either. After Driskell responded the way she did, it gave me so much hope for the future—both institutionally and personally.

Per the norm, that moment was indeed short-lived. After Driskell expressed her excitement and support for the idea, I don't think one minute passed before she queried, "Can you explore how to do this without a budget?"

And as quickly as the elation had me 30,000 feet in the air, it just as quickly had me plummet to the ground. "Umm, I'm not sure," I quietly stammered back.

She retorted, "We just don't have money in the budget right now, but this is great. You and Sallie figure out how to make this happen as best you can without more money. We just don't have it in the budget."

The message I heard then was, we don't have interest in prioritizing vision right now. We're focused on "CYA"[24] work only when it comes to Title IX and Equity. However, in a few short weeks, I would find out that wasn't the message at all. The message was actually, *"The budget" serves who we want it to serve when we want it served.*

How did this message come to fruition? Oh, thank you for asking–give me a brief moment to share. At this point, Laura was the Title IX Coordinator who would become the associate vice president of equity in January 2020. She was hired in 2018 through the search firm process; the same search firm that asked the VP of HR about putting me into the pool; the same VP of HR that voluntarily shared with me that she told them, "No, we've got something better for her."

So when she asked me if it could be done with no budget, only to later find out that within weeks of that meeting, Laura Johnson had been tasked with beginning the process of training and building restorative justice for the institution (later using it on her resume to interview for and acquire the position of AVP of equity), I was devastated. And to be quite honest, it may have been more shell shock and disbelief than anything. The institution was paying for a very experienced cohort of trainers to come in and train staff that worked with students institution-wide in preparation for implementing alternative resolutions. Laura would be leading the charge with no experience—I couldn't believe it.

Many moments like these tended to be the most painful and disconcerting because usually no one knew how badly I'd been wronged, and usually, it was messy and difficult to explain. So typically, I was forced to keep it to myself, internalize it, and do my best to move on and stay motivated. Usually questioning where I messed up, dropped the ball, missed the mark–doing my best to assume positive intent just to keep my sanity.

So when those two colleagues came to me sheepishly apologizing for how things were going down, it was a very unexpected validation that they saw how this played out without me having to plead my case to anyone willing to listen. It was little validating moments like that that would keep me from sinking into an abyss of discouragement and despair. Unbeknownst to Driskell, because those two colleagues were so curious about alternative resolution and knew my experience, they had been talking with me about it for weeks leading up to this.

In one of those conversations, I casually mentioned to them that I was going to pitch a position to Robyn so I could be dedicated to the work. So, it was little moments like that, had I not been in a relationship with them, they would have never known. Having that relationship allowed me a moment to be seen. Even when "the budget" was unavailable to allow me to be seen.

So, as the server in this restaurant shared more about the new stadium, she casually mentioned that it was working out great for the restaurant that Baylor wanted to relocate the stadium. "Baylor wanted to put fewer stadiums next to one another, so they decided to move the basketball stadium on this side of the highway instead."

Across the street, because the budget allowed.

Chapter 28: "Baal-or" University

Idol worship. Baal.[25] Western Christianity. As I read about Elijah and about the people's reactions and fervent defense of Baal, it became so obvious to me the way our modern day idols look. Christianity, nationalism, the flag, the Constitution, and Baylor are all gods that most Christians (people) respect, believe in, and follow at all costs. No matter what. And if you say or do anything not in alignment, things become aggressive and hostile *very* quickly.

The painful reality and reflection of the relationships I once called friends or even extended family–reflecting on how easy it was for them to bring us a meal, dine in our home, play with our children. But when forced to examine the loyalties to their idols, namely Baylor—they always choose their idol. Their idols are familiar. Their idol is safety. Their idol is comfortable.

From some friends, we'd hear them say, "It's just heartbreaking what the Wardlaws went through with Baylor." and "That's just terrible." Or "I totally believe what she says happened," as they sit in the stadium to cheer on their beloved *Bears*.

For others, they would rather move on with their lives and pretend they were never in a relationship with us. They would function as if we literally went rogue–formulating theories about our "rebellious behavior" that helps them sleep better at night. Hoping to move on with their lives with as little disruption as possible, but filling in the gaps of the friendship where they can.

Looking to continue their lives as seamlessly as possible. The comforts of normalcy, and dare I say complicity, are much safer and palatable than stepping out on a limb to pause to consider the legitimacy of the Wardlaws' grievances with their idol.

Chapter 29: The Black Woman, Strong

Many of us know her all too well.
She's the mom. The grandma. The sister. The friend. The go-to. Because she's relentless.
Steady. Focused. Intimidating. Intense.
Sharp with the mind and the tongue.
Whatever she touches brings fruit.
She's Eve.
She's you. She's me.
I'm writing to you, strong black woman. For all the times you've been told you're too intense.
You need to calm down.
You've been denigrated or humiliated for someone else to be taller, smarter, stronger, brighter.
You are. You are. You are.
Your presence shifts nations. Your presence builds dynasties. Your presence brings hope. Your presence brings life.
And no matter what or who tries to take life from you, know that you are life. And no amount of oppression can change that.
So when you walk away. When you choose to fight. When you choose to sit. When you choose to stand. When you choose to leave quietly. When you choose to leave loudly. Know that space will never be the same.
You're not missing it or missing out. They are.

They've missed the opportunity to walk hand and hand with greatness. No need to convince. Just know that you are.

And nothing more has to be said.

***

This was inspired by a dear friend and sister of mine who is walking an all-too-familiar road. *May you always know your worth and be reminded of the treasure that you are.*

Chapter 30: To Sue or Not to Sue

What's the end goal, they ask? My answer: liberation.

I've often wrestled with this idea of bringing a "landmark" case against Baylor University. I've thought about the cost in money, the cost in time, and the cost in my psyche. And I just have to ask, is it worth it? What many people don't realize is the toll that's paid in bringing a lawsuit, especially against a deep-pocket institution like Baylor University.

It seems like Avengers Endgame—the likelihood of success is 14 million to 1. And then I can't help but think about my ancestors and sojourners who have gone before me, bringing landmark cases that changed history in its tracks. I wrestled and wrestled—should I or shouldn't I?

I think about the Harriet Tubmans who didn't stop at their own liberation—they went back to free others.[26] I recognize the pain that came with her liberation and then the sacrifices she made to bring others freedom as well. It cost her her husband. It cost her friends. It cost her others lives. And I wrestled. Not willing to forgo doing the right thing for my comforts. But focused on discerning the right thing no matter the cost.

I get frustrated thinking about how I didn't get to tell my story to the investigators. How my attorney reminded me that the investigator is hired by Baylor, paid by Baylor, and ultimately wants more contracts from Baylor. A white firm. With white investigators. Who live in a white world. With white respondents (accused) and white witnesses who are still paid by Baylor. What reason do they have to make a finding for me? Baylor would then have everything they need to protect themselves against me in the event I do bring a lawsuit.

Then I'm reminded of the psychologically broken down claimants that sat in my office week after week, semester after semester, year after year. Fearful and hesitant to even come forward—believing what I know to be true—they never had a fighting chance. The policy is not written to support them, and ultimately the systems are not built to support them.

So for every claimant that still went through the process, I give a standing ovation for your courage and a heartfelt apology for your pain. For every claimant who walked away knowing it was a zero-sum game for them, I give a standing ovation for your courage and a heartfelt apology for your pain.

My hands are bloody, and I want to make it right. I operated weapons I didn't know were lethal. They were lethal to me and every person of color who walked through the doors of the "Equity Office."

My colleague and I used to look at our jobs in the Equity office like hospice. If you're coming to us, it's so bad at this point that it's likely over for you. So we'll do our best to keep you comfortable and make this process as painless as possible. But I now realize more than ever that it wasn't just hospice - it was euthanasia. And the thought of working in that space, doing that work at the hands of that institution, makes me want to vomit.

And to actually think I could stomach maintaining friendships with people who say or think, "What's your endgame?" is unimaginable. If you cannot see or discern what I have seen, experienced, or felt and can't understand why or how I've done or am doing what I am—we literally have nothing to talk about. This is warfare, and your ignorance will cost me my life, as well as your own.

Yes, Harriet went back to free others. But they had to be willing to run for their lives. They had to be willing to lay it all down in the hope of liberation. They knew in their souls that they desired liberation, and when given the chance to have it— they ran like hell.

So will I sue? Probably not. That may or may not be my lane. Will I talk? Hell yeah... My voice, my words, my story *will* liberate others. Just like having the freedom to tell, it has liberated me.

Chapter 31: Status and Street Cred

So one thing that often perplexes me, and some of what I share throughout this book, runs at a cross-section of our exit from both the church and workplace institution. But as I've reflected on our popularity, or even notoriety while in Waco, it was truly nothing short of divine. While I was hired in somewhat of a high profile position because of the state of Baylor University when it came to Title IX in 2016/2017, I wasn't hired in a position where an announcement was made or published in any way.

So to think about the recognizability that we gained so quickly and so plausibly, it literally was divine. It was to the point that I would want so badly just to get where I was going and not be stopped, so I would look extra busy and not make eye contact.

But even if people didn't actually know us, they were very motivated to get to know us. This resulted in a lot of connections, and a lot of unexpected relationships formed at farmers markets, grocery stores, playgrounds, you name it. We had a lot of respect from people very quickly. So much so that it landed us square on the front page of the Wacoan, a local magazine that everyone in the city has access to. Well written and put together, but mass distributed.

A local journalist interviewed us, and we had the opportunity to tell our story of how we even got to Waco! And even though it felt like we were rambling, people told us over and over again how inspiring it was to them. To hear of the giant leap of faith it was to come here and the challenges that have ensued, but how Gary and I have remained a team was a testimony to the community. But even the way people have rallied around us, it was extremely comforting because we didn't have family around, and were somewhat displaced.

So what has been really interesting to me both at Baylor and with the church, never once did we say, "Man, we would sure love to blow up our popularity and sacrifice all of the connections we've made." Says no one ever.

So to me, it *begs* the question, why would you all do that if it were not for something Spirit-led and that you felt strongly convicted about? I wonder why these people that we have adored, and dare I say, revered, sacrificed it all to say things that no one wants to hear? That no one wants to believe. That most people want to ignore.

Because it's what's right. It's liberating. And it sets the captives free. We may be sacrificing but it's for the greater good. But it still makes me want to stand on top of the Alico building and yell, "If you respected and loved us so much, why doesn't it make you stop and say, 'Hmm, this is the Wardlaws. And I don't think they would do or say the things they're saying if there wasn't something to it. That's just not how they roll…'"

Putting something like this on paper requires boldness. Courage. Confidence. And unwavering sight on the Father–divine foresight. Whether or not you believe in prophecy, I'll tell you this–everything we're walking in right now was prophesied to me several years ago. It scared me because it all seemed so much out of my comfort zone.

Now here we are, exceedingly abundantly above what we could have asked or imagined.

But I understand more than ever what it was like to walk in Jesus' shoes. Not from what I heard in church or Sunday school but from actually following where the Spirit has led, even if it meant sacrificing it all. And it has led to being the most loved and hated family in Waco in a few years' time. Jesus knows a bit about what that's like. When you start speaking truth to religious people who believe the church starts and ends with them, it's not pretty. And you may find yourself the most loved and hated individual within the same week. It ain't popular. And it doesn't feel great. But it absolutely feels right. Especially when those marginalized people who have been living in the shadows start to come out because they've been too ashamed, afraid, or unnoticed.

But no one seems to make this connection on their own because no one wants to be compared to the religious people of Jesus' time. We're blinded by that connection.

Have our religious clothes changed? A little, I guess. Have our religious practices changed? A little, I guess. Has our religious language changed? A little, I guess. But at the heart of the religious practice, responses, expectations, and attitudes—*the same*. But because no one wants to be a Pharisee, they refuse to make the connection. Blinded by how Americanized Western comfortable, robotic, and predictable Christianity is the modern-day contemporary of Jewish leaders in Jesus' day.

They think because they're polite and smile, they're like Jesus. The Jesus I know dined with sinners. He brought the people healing which resulted in the gospel. *Freedom and healing*. That's the foundation of the Jesus and gospel I know.

Chapter 32: When I Knew It Was Over

As I mentioned, believe it or not, I had a serious boyfriend before Gary—Tavion. Yes, there was a before Gary. And you couldn't have convinced me Tavion wasn't my forever. We did what most teenage, young adults do in relationships—the break-up, get back together cycle for years. Now granted, I was never the person who broke up over a spat because I'm typically not spontaneous or impulsive with my emotions. When we did break up, it was for at least six months to a year before we found our way back to this "relationship."

The last time we got back together and broke up, I was a 2L in law school. Not a freshman or sophomore in college. Not a junior or senior in college. Why does that matter? What was so different about this particular point of my life? Well, I was changing in significant ways. I had begun law school, hopeful of my future as a successful lawyer, but quickly realized that I was in need of a much deeper motivation to get me through. I needed more purpose.

And in a breaking moment for me 1L year God spoke to me clearly that I was going to use this degree to "be a voice to the voiceless." To speak up for those who could not speak up for themselves (*Proverbs 31:8-9*). But little did I know that this was going to be a decade long journey of first learning to speak up for myself. To find my own voice. And as I said, that process began to rapidly unfold in law school.

So, what does this beau have to do with finding my voice? Well, like I said, by law school, I was changing. I always thought I was pretty confident, but my intellectual insecurities were being highlighted and exposed. I had to constantly battle with the intrusive thoughts of inadequacy and incompetence. I would sit in class holding back tears because I was hearing things in my head like, *Why are you here?*

You know you can't do this!

These people are so much smarter than you.

I even had to work through a handful of black people in my class calling me "the black blonde" behind my back (talk about middle school trauma all over again!). It was three of the hardest years for me psychologically. But in the midst of those years, the summer after 2L year, I found myself back in this relationship, after previously breaking up shortly before law school had started.

But something was different this time. While it was nice to be with the familiar again in hopes that this was our final lap to marriage, something seemed a little off.

We talked about the visit with him in his hometown of Birmingham where he had made a lot of plans around things he knew I'd enjoy—picnics by the pond, visits to the Civil Rights museums, romantic dinners at the Cheesecake Factory. While I didn't really have to pressure him into doing any of these things, I was pretty aware that he was miserable doing them.

Nothing about any of these things excited him. And while it was subtle, I eventually had that epiphany when I knew that nothing about doing these things with someone who was tangentially interested, was sustainable. But I pushed through for a time. Why? Because we had been at this for so many years, we looked great in photos together, and this was supposed to work!

My hair. A defining intersection. In both relationships (beau and Baylor), the straightened, blown out, flowy, and, dare I say, "European-like" hair was adored. My blowouts were top-notch. It didn't matter if it was a bob, or if my length game was on point, or even if I was rocking the Halle Berry meets Megan Goode. I was fly. And everyone else knew it, too.

However, everyone also knew that it will likely look exceptionally different within weeks, whether it was color or scissors—I'm always liable to switch it up. But it was in both relationships, beau and Baylor, that there were switch ups that were too far outside their level of comfort with me. With my ex, it was going natural. With Baylor, it was color and scissors. They both felt very entitled to feel very strongly about what was an appropriate expression of myself with my hair.

When Tavion and I got back together this last time, I had recently discovered how beautiful my natural hair was! I was embarking full speed, away from the creamy crack.[27] But he didn't hide his distaste for my natural styles. As dating couples do, we sent pictures to one another on days we knew we were cute but wouldn't see one another. But without fail, if I sent a picture and my hair was natural, he was completely unresponsive. The silence was deafening.

With Baylor, it was the purple and then the "Grace Jones" pixy. And ironically, the purple was actually a major misstep at the time. I never intended for it to be as purple as it ended up. While I was scared to death of what it would do to my career, God spoke very clearly and said, "You're entering a season of *bold* and *unconventional*."

I remember very vividly having a conversation with a dear friend at the time—a high up, middle-aged white woman who worked for Baylor—and she was concerned or questioned my judgment on making a decision like that knowing how it could/would impact my career.

And while she was right, this was the beginning of recognizing how often we as black people leave aspects of ourselves at the door to make everyone inside feel more comfortable. Expressions of our creativity are boxed and suppressed for their comfort and approval.

A few months later, I decided it was time for a cut. But, like the color, the cut I had in mind was not nearly as drastic as what the barber executed. Ushering me yet again into a much bolder expression than I intended. And yet again, another situation that exposed the times that we have to leave part of ourselves at the door to make everyone else inside more comfortable.

And it showed. In spite of demonstrating my best performance since I had been at the institution, with creative new ideas and execution of various visions and major projects—I had dyed my hair purple and got a haircut that made people question my alignment or allyship with the LGBTQ community. As I shared, in spite of my performance, this resulted in not only a denial of the promotion I was promised at the inception of my role with EEO and equity but the total dismissal for even a first-round consideration.

Our last fight, I knew it was really over. But it was exactly the closure I needed to know it was really over. Honestly, there was nothing really atypical about this fight. In years past, we would have a disagreement, we would attempt to have a conversation about it, he would shut down, not speak to me for a few days, I would make a few attempts to talk again through text or call, be ignored, and when he was ready, he'd come back around and we would pretend like nothing happened and move on.

As a 19 to 20-year-old, this was OK, and I was just happy to stay together. It didn't matter if we didn't resolve anything, it didn't matter if we didn't make space to communicate and understand one another, it didn't matter if my opinions were never expressed, it didn't matter that the stress and anxiety and wondering when he would speak to me again gave me stomach ulcers. All that mattered was that we were speaking again. Even if it meant glossing over things that should have mattered.

So fast forward a few years to this fight, this now 3L who had been finding her voice, recognizing it's value, understanding and believing her opinions mattered, understanding the psychological defeat of being silenced, learning how to speak up no matter how uncomfortable it was for the status quo—the reality that this dynamic in any relationship was no longer acceptable or sustainable. It didn't matter how much I had invested over the years.

It didn't matter how good we looked together. Or if it made sense on paper... It didn't matter how much they were paying me or that working at a well-known institution was something to be desired. It didn't matter that this was what I was "supposed" to do—meet an attractive college athlete and get married; it didn't matter if I went along with the status quo for the marginalized. I wouldn't ruffle feathers and can be better positioned for a promotion. It didn't matter that finding myself and my voice made you uncomfortable.

What does matter is that I do have a voice. I am creative. I am brilliant. I'm unaccepting of the status quo. I have opinions. I believe in justice. I believe in doing what's right no matter the cost. I believe that the Lord fights for me. I believe the Lord loves justice. I believe the Lord fights for justice. And I believe that good will always triumph over evil. And I believe my voice matters.

So, I knew it was over when the message and expectations were apparent—we need you to lower, squelch or silence your voice altogether. The sooner you do that, the sooner we'll feel more comfortable about this relationship. Both Baylor and my ex's disdain for my voice and expression, began to be apparent.

Their clear frustration with the new Brittney and for their clear nostalgic desire for the old Brittney who focused more on navigating their discomfort and doing backbends and acrobatic stunts to keep them at peace. She was slowly becoming more and more unavailable. Why? Because she was finding her voice in order to speak up for those who could not speak for themselves.

So I think we all knew things were coming to an end. This is not the Brittney they remembered, nor the one they desired. So, really, we only had one option—to part ways. Because *this* Brittney has work to do. And there was no need to waste any more of one another's time because this was no longer practical or sustainable.

Chapter 33: Thank You & Farewell

I realized how often Gary and I have been exorbitantly intentional about telling people thank you and giving warm, lavish public appreciation. I think we've always been that way for as long as I can remember. I'm not sure if it was a shift in my heart of the why behind the thank yous *or* if I've just recently become more acutely aware of my heart in the thank yous. Operating in freedom is a funny thing. Until you're free, sometimes you don't even realize how much bondage you were actually in. We learn to operate in bondage because it's familiar.

It reminds me of those Israelites. And the more unfamiliar and unsure things got, the more they longed to go back to Egypt to bondage. So going back to thinking through the why we offered intentional, outspoken thank yous, I can only speak for myself in examining the why as Gary is on his own journey as well. But for me, I'm realizing more and more that there was something in me that inherently felt a weighty responsibility or obligation to make sure that those who helped or supported me felt extremely appreciated and celebrated for doing so. Almost as if I was afraid of losing their support as if they were our sustainers. And at times, it did feel that way.

We hit some rough patches physically and financially in Waco, and the support was undeniable. So remembering those individuals and even organizations that met many of our physical needs created this sense of obligation or allegiance. A different form of bondage. One I'm realizing, as the chains begin to break in so many areas of my life, has always been a place of bondage for me. Regardless of a person's motives for being there for me, supporting me in some way—I've always operated as if I owe them something.

Knowing I can't give back what they gave me, the least I could do is sing their praises, very verbosely and publicly, so that I know they feel appreciated. Leave a lavish thank-you gift. Or at least write a beautifully thoughtful thank you note.

Whether it has been my parents, a church, or even God. A total paradigm shift in my mind, in my relationships, and even in understanding my relationship with my Savior. Challenging something deep, deep within that says, you did _____ for me, I at *least* have to _____. But there's a staunch difference between offering gratitude as a symbol of appreciation and feeling like gratitude is owed.

As I become more mindful and aware of what I feel and what I'm experiencing, this bondage was revealed to me as I would think about the specific individuals who really went above and beyond to assist us in our darkest hours over the years. With the breakup from Baylor and the breakup from Antioch, there were natural breakups that happened with individuals and families. Whether it was people who just didn't understand our stance, didn't agree with our approach, or just preferred not to be associated with controversy, the breakups happened.

And when I would reflect on these individuals, there would be emotions that arose, namely anxiety. A sense of angst and obligation to these individuals. "Aw man, they've done so much for us... how can I make sure they know we're grateful for what they did..." and a whole lot of other conflicting, binding, and restricting feelings that have frequently and significantly inhibited my ability to run and fly in the direction of God's leading—whether speaking, writing, or recording.

And that's when it hit me. The lie I believed was that these people "provided for us" and "we owed" them _____. The truth is God provided for us through countless individuals. He can use anyone. At any time. And we do not owe these individuals anything, but a "thank you for your obedience." Not out of obligation, but from my perspective as encouragement of their privilege to be a part of something bigger than themselves.

And I want to be clear, I don't know or even think people expected what I thought I owed. But acknowledging the bondage for me, created another opportunity to operate in freedom. And free is where He has called us to be.

Chapter 34: The Two Shall Become One

The gentle, yet strong; the broken, yet unwavering look he would have in his eyes was what I remember vividly throughout my time at Baylor.

With any new opportunity that was on the horizon—whether it was a project, an idea, or a promotion, he brought hope, enthusiasm, and a motivational speech with all of his heart and belief. And every time I was rejected, denied, chastised, and gaslit, he fought to hold space for my anxiety and feelings of insufficiency. He chose to show up hopeful and motivating in spite of his real pain for what he watched me endure year after year, work day after work day.

As the one who was going into an office every day enduring the psychological warfare, I think I took for granted his own psychological battle that was underway. He was supposed to be my covering, yet he watched me leave the house every day and was still doing an incredible job of displaying hope and motivation for us both to keep enduring and believing that this move was not in vain.

Every foggy memory I have that flickered in the caverns of trauma in my mind, he can recall with great precision and detail. Details that still baffle me with disbelief that I and many others weathered as long as we did. And as much as he didn't think he did or was able to protect me, he did that and much more.

He created and nurtured a home base. It was always a safe haven and reprieve. He took the painful jabs from family, friends, and foes who questioned his position. Questioning whether his supporting me from home, caring for our small children, navigating our finances, affirming my competence and abilities, and seeking community in a foreign land as a marginalized human being was really practical, appropriate, or even Biblical.

A heavily licensed and degreed, black male stay-at-home parent in the Central Texas Baptist Bible Belt south. With two kids under three. And a wife who was the primary and only "breadwinner." The most unsung hero in this story.

Yet every day, some days fighting depression and utter psychological and emotional exhaustion, he found a way to nurture this haven. He managed to bring my newborn and infants to campus, everyday—multiple times a day, so Mommy could feed and not have to take the extra time to pump (and this was long before hands free pumps were the norm). He managed to have a home-cooked meal for dinner daily. He grocery shopped, cleaned, counseled, carpooled, and classroom volunteered—mostly without community.

He managed to think of and implement creative homeschool activities, teaching our toddler all 66 books of the Bible. And not to mention he managed to teach himself how to do their beautiful black hair from intuition and YouTube. And vlog along the way.

So when I say that those gentle yet affirming, steady yet unwavering eyes were not to be forgotten—I mean that from the depths of my soul—a place that now overflows with gratitude for the sacrifices he made and the steady and concrete support he has had for me.

Many may know about the Ph.D. program at James Madison University that this 'A' student left to support me in a new role, with a newborn, as a stay-at-home dad. And even though I tried to insist he stay back and finish—it was that same gentle yet unwavering look he gave and matter-of-factly stated, "Absolutely not... if we're going, we're going together."

And while my deepest fear was always that he would later resent me when we watched his cohort post their degrees and graduation pictures two years later, he never wavered. And even if he did, those same steady, gentle, and unwavering eyes never told me otherwise.

The commitment and theme of our marriage have cemented through the years. Neither one of us could have known that our wedding scripture, Genesis 2:24, would be a firm foundation for us on the journey ahead. "For this reason, a man will leave his father and mother and be united to his wife, and they will become one flesh."

And that Ruth 1:16, "...Don't urge me to leave you or to turn back from you. Where you go I will go, and where you stay I will stay..." would also be a critical load-bearing structure of our sacred union.

Both are undeniably a vow and a testament to our marital story. And walking these roads together has cemented a bond—three strands that are not easily broken (Ecclesiastes 4:12).

Chapter 35: Elevation with Purpose

Esther was in the palace with a purpose. We can't get so comfortable with our elevated status that we forget why we're there and elevated. It's tempting to get comfortable, settle in, and set up camp. Gary and I often joke that as soon as we hang decorations, build a new and comfortable community, or even plant a garden—God says, "Time to go!"

The temptation is to reason with God about better timing or plead to stick around and enjoy the fruit a little longer, but we've come to realize that there's greater reward in moving with Him, rather than trying to hang around where He once was.

Chapter 36: Would I Go Back if I Could?

I sometimes ponder to myself what it would be like to go back to Lynchburg or even work at Liberty again. I sometimes replay interactions or situations that happened at Baylor, contemplating how I would respond now. Usually, these reflections make me shake my head and move to the next, more important thought, or I literally laugh out loud. But the spring from which the laugh erupts is incredibly telling of not only my status of wholeness but also so richly reflective.

I used to think, *There's no way I could go back and not get fired*. But I've since realized that the power I now possess is something that no person, man or woman, white or black, churchgoer or atheist, can take away from me. You can't forget the flavor of freedom. There are no words to describe the liberated mind, heart, or body. I laugh, knowing the reach of my wingspan takes me beyond anywhere I realized then I was capable of going.

I'm far smarter, far wiser, far more creative than I ever knew I could be. If I went back to those spaces, it would have to be under at least one of these circumstances—an institution or organization that knows and hopes for the greatest of me, or I am flying contained on purpose and with purpose. Not from a place of fear and suffocating circumstances but purely from informed choice and calculated intentionality.

"Where the Spirit of the Lord is... there is Liberty" (2 Corinthians 3:17). When you walked into the atrium of the main academic building on Liberty's campus, you could see this verse beautifully scribed on the wall below the massive and ornate ceilings. I read it often. Every time I headed to the computer lab for some "late night studying" or headed to my computer management information systems class. I even remember reading it over and over again as I stood next to Jerry Falwell Sr.'s lifeless body holding a tissue box as thousands of people from across the campus and nation paid their respects.

This peculiar leadership assignment post afforded me a lot of reflection time as I watched all of these people that his vision had impacted. At some point, I remember thinking, *Hmmm... that verse is very befitting. Did he get the name from the verse or identify the verse as a good fit for his vision? Nevertheless, it works.*

As my path has weaved and wound over the last couple of decades, it has become clearer and clearer how much of the things and people I've seen and crossed paths with were not quite what they once appeared to be.

When the roads lead you and leave you feeling like the diamonds and gold are nothing but sequins and plastic glitter, you sometimes spend some time in the dark—wrestling with cynicism and hopelessness. But if you keep walking, you see that beyond the darkness, there is light. If we don't give up, lean in, and follow that glimmer of light, it will eventually lead to freedom. It did for me.

That verse that Liberty and the Falwells effectively used to capitalize on a highly monetizable vision, the ways that business and capitalism were married to religion and tradition, could leave us all feeling jaded and forever put off by Christianity. But, if we refuse to stop there, lean a little more, walk a little further, and refuse to lose sight of the light in our darkest hour, we all may find that hope and freedom are at the end of the road.

I could have never known that the verse that I had once read over and over and once saw as a means to manipulative gain would awaken something new—that in my darkest and most despondent hours, I leaned a little further, pressed in a little harder and read the more complete story.

Now the Lord is the Spirit, and where the Spirit of the Lord is, there is freedom. And we, who with unveiled faces all reflect the Lord's glory, are being transformed into his likeness with ever-increasing glory, which comes from the Lord, who is the Spirit (2 Corinthians 3:17-18).

God is writing my story, and my story didn't end where it could have. And neither does yours. I've been leaning and continue to lean. And if we don't lose sight of that glimmer of light and follow the road where that light is leading, it will lead us out of the darkness. The journey is not an easy one. But it's also not one we should quit if we want to be free. As we follow that light, we will be transformed into His likeness with ever-increasing glory.

Chapter 37: To All of You Who Thought You Knew What You Didn't Know You Thought You Knew

If it was about getting a raise, I would have left after I was denied an opportunity to interview for one during my first year at Baylor.

I like following rules. I do not enjoy disrupting regularly scheduled programs and expectations.

I want to give my deepest apologies and most sincere "I am so sorry" to every complainant, black and brown, that came to my office and told me you were called a nigger or you heard the word used on the job, and I told you that didn't meet the burden of proof for a hostile work environment.

I'm so sorry to the Latin complainant who came to my office to tell me that the faculty members that chased you down to ask you if you were excited about the catered tacos, beans and rice, could not be held responsible for how they regularly made you feel–failing to treat you as the esteemed educator that you are.

To every black colleague who was made to feel uncomfortable by my "disruptive" departure, can I remind you of what Dr. King once said? "Nonviolent direct action seeks to create such a crisis and establish such creative tension that a community that has constantly refused to negotiate is forced to confront the issue."

To my Black friends that felt they were left to dry, I did my best to make hard decisions that would eventually leave those left behind in better positions. From the documents I disclosed, the hard conversations I had in my mediations and negotiations, and the names I dropped. It was always intended to be for the greater good of all.

Money would have helped our family tremendously. From moving expenses four times over, from student loan debt to losing my public service loan forgiveness, to being a one-income family, to taking a job under the auspice of paid maternity leave. I never took a dollar.

I did always want a raise. Would more money be nice? Of course. But the primary objective was more influence, more power to have the ability to advocate for the change I knew Baylor needed to make to live up to the ideals they purported to have.

We were not living in sin or outside of God's will when my husband stayed home with our children while I obeyed a call we both heard. He was actually being a bigger man than most are willing to be by making the ultimate sacrifice to obey the Lord and serve and care for his family well.

If you felt like you needed to walk away from being in community with us, don't feel bad—you're in good company. It happened to people in the Bible all the time.

If you tried to stay in community with us and felt like we resisted, the truth is—we may have. We either weren't sure if you could be trusted, or we needed time to heal. Or both.

If you stood by and didn't use your voice to advocate for us, know that at the time, it looked and felt cowardly. Now, we have more grace to recognize that we are all in different spaces at different times. If you're at peace with your decision, so are we.

For every co-worker and supervisor who questioned my intellectual abilities before a time when wireless pumping was a thing, please know I had to stop my work three to four times a day to hook up to a breast pump, store the milk, and wipe down my equipment and meet the same deadlines; while nursing a child at night that didn't sleep for longer than 90-minute stretches, and then be expected to come to an office every day and fire on all cylinders.

Should I have had different representation/counsel? Was my attorney aggressive, unpolished, and rough around the edges? To most, yes. Was he the only attorney within 250 miles that I had access to who wasn't afraid or intimidated by Baylor? Who didn't claim to "have a conflict?" Yes.

To everyone who's wondering what happened to those Wardlaws—the headline is, we're free. We're thriving. And we're overwhelmed with gratitude.

Conclusion

As I wrote the contents of this book, unpacking the interactions, the experiences and revelations of what I understood to be happening, I often queried—what is the purpose and the goal? Ultimately, I knew it was for liberation. But for who? How? And I realize more now than ever before. It's for me. It's for you. We are all called and created to be free.

I was doing a devotional Bible study with a small group we recently joined. Many of the principles were truths I needed to revisit as I had spent much of the last couple of years deconstructing and reconsidering much of what I had been taught from white evangelical teaching. Because of the pain and brokenness that both my husband and I experienced at their hands, we had found ourselves abandoning much of what we had learned for fear that they had manipulated Christianity to be self-serving, keeping the oppressor in power and the oppressed in submission. It was a scary time.

I had never gone so long as not to pick up my Bible. Not to step foot in a church. Not to have reflective and meditative time in prayer. But as the Lord wooed me back to Him and reconstructed the truth of who He is, I found my way back to the word. Having truths of the word illuminated *directly* to me. Noticing and reading Scripture that I felt I had never even seen before! How was this even possible? I'd read this Bible of mine cover to cover multiple times in my life.

And I found myself asking, "Now, where did that verse come from?!" It felt good to rebuild. It felt good to be reintroduced to my dearest friend in a new and beautiful way. But it took courage and obedience to respond to the woo and allow Him the time and space to heal me.

So as I started the devotional Bible study, it was a hearty meal to my hungry soul. I would be remiss not to say that at times, some of how the study was written was triggering. Reminding me of the language and culture of the white evangelical nomenclature I was bred and nurtured in. However, I came to realize that I had an opportunity before me. I could allow the enemy to do what he does, which is steal.

Or I could take the next step and trust the Lord to illuminate to me what He had for me in the text—beyond any seeds of resentment, bitterness or anger that were trying to take root. And as a result, God has continued to speak life to me in a way that only He could. A healing and liberating way.

I recently came across a question in the devotional that said, "Have you ever persistently prayed for something and not received it or received something different? Briefly describe one of those experiences." My answer was a resounding yes. You see, this entire story was one of those experiences. When I turned down an opportunity to get a promotion as an executive leader over equity in Virginia and left Liberty University to be at Baylor, I had expectations of a similar opportunity at some point once I arrived.

I didn't know how long it would be but I ultimately resolved to trust God with the process because I had loved my journey thus far. In my mind, not a problem, He can be trusted right? And despite the tumultuous ride when we landed in Waco, I was still praying and believing that the Lord was paving my path and preparing me to be an executive over equity there.

I was so passionate and felt deeply called to this role. In my mind, *this* is how we bring liberation to the marginalized at the institution, both students and staff. This is where I have the opportunity to do what I love, enjoy, and feel fire and giftings to do.

"Lord, I will continue to pray for *this* role because this is exactly how I will liberate others!" And as the doors seemingly opened and then shut year after year, I thought I was called to persevere. My time was coming... right? Right. But not in the way that I assumed. I was called to help others be liberated. But first, I had to be free myself. Freed from the chains in my heart and in my mind. God had a much better way of doing this. I thought the way to do it was from the inside.

So as I prayed for this AVP of equity role inside the confines of the plantation, the Lord said, "I hear your prayer and agree with you. But your finite understanding of liberation is limiting... and I've got a bigger and better way to do this. Just trust me."

So here I stand. Healed, whole, and on the outside of the plantation. Using my voice to speak truth and life to the captives. Where is God wanting to free you and others beyond your limited understanding of how to do it? Did the Lord answer my prayer? Absolutely. Did He answer the way that I thought He would? Absolutely not. And as a result, I'm more free and more whole than I ever could have imagined.

I am praying that sharing my experiences goes beyond giving the "T" of what went down when I was at Baylor. That it goes beyond airing my grievances and gives another the courage to take the brave steps toward freedom and a liberated existence...

Appendix

Notes

Part 1: Run Aground Road

1. Amend — Chapter 1: Truth

A documentary series directed by Kenny Leon and Reinaldo Marcus Green. Hosted by Will Smith, we explore the ongoing struggle for equal rights in America. It shines a light on the 14th Amendment of the US Constitution, a key part that ensures fairness for all. Through stories of brave individuals who fought for justice, the show reveals how this amendment has shaped American democracy. It's a journey into history and modern times, showing why the 14th Amendment remains vital in upholding our country's core values of liberty and justice for everyone.

Amend: The Fight for America. 2021. Netflix.

2. "White Supremacy" — Chapter 1: Truth

White supremacy is a system that favors white people and their beliefs, often at the expense of people of color. It's about maintaining power and privilege for white elites, often through oppression and exploitation. This system has deep historical roots and continues to be upheld by institutions in society.

Annie Jaffee and Zachary A. Casey. "White Supremacy." In *Encyclopedia of Critical Whiteness Studies in Education*, 694-702. Brill, 2020. https://brill.com/display/book/9789004444836/BP000099.xml

3. An "ally" — Chapter 2: Allies and Friends

The concept of allyship involves individuals from one social identity group supporting members of another group, typically with a member of the dominant group advocating for those facing discrimination or injustice, irrespective of their own identity. This collaborative effort towards addressing prejudice and discrimination in society yields collective benefits for all involved.

What does it mean to be an ally? Ontario Public Service Employees Union, 2015. PDF. https://opseu.org/wp-content/uploads/2015/10/what_does_it_mean_to_be_an_ally.pdf

4. "Big joker" — Chapter 2: Allies and Friends

In traditional card games, particularly those like Euchre or certain variations of Poker, the Joker card holds a unique position. Often depicted as a court jester, clown, or harlequin, it symbolizes traits such as chaos, unpredictability, wit, and intelligence. When both Jokers are utilized, they typically function as the highest-ranking trump cards in the game. Within the spade suit, which typically consists of 15 cards, the Big Joker, also known as the Full-Color Joker, holds a superior position to the Little Joker, or One-Color Joker. Notably, the Big Joker outranks even the ace of spades, emphasizing its significance and dominance within the hierarchy of the card deck.

"Spades with Jokers," *Bicycle*. Retrieved from https://bicyclecards.com/how-to-play/spades-with-jokers

Ryan Joyce, "Joker Card Meaning: The Mysterious Origins," *Learn Magic*, May 2023. Retrieved from https://www.magicianmasterclass.com/post/joker-card#:~:text=The%20Joker%20card%20is%20often,symbol%20of%20chaos%20and%20cunning

5. "The Body Keeps the Score..." — Chapter 2: Allies and Friends

"The Body Keeps the Score" by Bessel van der Kolk explores how trauma affects the body and mind, emphasizing that traumatic experiences can leave deep physical and psychological scars. The book discusses how trauma disrupts the brain's ability to process emotions and memories, often leading to physical ailments and mental health issues. It integrates neuroscience, psychology, and personal stories to highlight the importance of understanding and treating trauma through approaches like therapy, mindfulness, and yoga, aiming to help individuals reclaim their lives and well-being.

Van der Kolk, Bessel A. *The Body Keeps the Score: Brain, Mind, and Body in the Healing of Trauma.* Phoenix, AZ: Milton H. Erickson Foundation, 2014.

6. Asian hate — Chapter 2: Allies and Friends

"Stop Asian Hate" is a slogan that demonstrations, protests, and rallies held across the United States to combat violence against Asians, Asian Americans, and others of Asian descent. These events were in response to the surge in racial discrimination against Asian Americans during the COVID-19 pandemic. As the virus spread, reports of racially motivated hate crimes involving physical violence and harassment against Asian Americans increased. Historically, health crises have often led to the stigmatization and "othering" of people of Asian descent. Asian Americans have faced verbal and physical violence driven by racism and xenophobia. At the institutional level, the state has often implicitly supported this violence through bigoted rhetoric and exclusionary policies. The COVID-19 pandemic has exacerbated racism, contributing to national insecurity, fear of foreigners, and general xenophobia, which may explain the rise in anti-Asian hate crimes during this period. This examination highlights how these crimes, rooted in long-standing individual and institutional racism and xenophobia, have perpetuated the "othering" of Asian Americans and reinforced inequality.

Gover, A.R., Harper, S.B. & Langton, L. Anti-Asian Hate Crime During the COVID-19 Pandemic: Exploring the Reproduction of Inequality. Am J Crim Just 45, 647–667 (2020). https://doi.org/10.1007/s12103-020-09545-1.

7. MOU — Chapter 3: Pet to Threat

A memorandum of understanding (MOU) is an agreement between two or more parties that outlines their shared intentions and plans for working together. It specifies each party's roles, responsibilities, and expectations, aiming to ensure everyone is on the same page. The purpose of an MOU is to create a clear understanding of the partnership, setting the stage for a future enforceable contract that all parties are comfortable with.

"What Is a Memorandum of Understanding (MOU) and How Do You Write One?" Web log. *Adobe* (blog), n.d. https://www.adobe.com/acrobat/business/resources/memorandum-of-understanding.html.

8. Imposter Syndrome — Chapter 3: Pet to Threat

Imposter syndrome (IS) is a behavioral health phenomenon described as self-doubt of intellect, skills, or accomplishments among high-achieving individuals. These individuals cannot internalize their success and subsequently experience pervasive feelings of self-doubt, anxiety, depression, and/or apprehension of being exposed as a fraud in their work, despite verifiable and objective evidence of their successfulness. The terms imposter syndrome and imposter phenomenon (IP) are used interchangeably, with IP gaining more frequent use in recent literature. Imposter syndrome was first described in 1978 by Suzanne Imes, Ph.D., and Pauline Rose Clance, Ph.D. as an observation first among successful women and other marginalized groups.

Huecker MR, Shreffler J, McKeny PT, et al. Imposter Phenomenon. Updated 2023 Jul 31. In: StatPearls. Treasure Island (FL): StatPearls Publishing; 2024 Jan-. Available from: https://www.ncbi.nlm.nih.gov/books/NBK585058/.

9. EEO — Chapter 2: Allies and Friends

Equal Employment Opportunity (EEO) laws are designed to prevent job discrimination in specific workplaces. These laws ensure that all employees and job applicants receive fair treatment regardless of race, color, religion, sex, national origin, age, disability, or genetic information. The U.S. Department of Labor (DOL) oversees the enforcement and monitoring of EEO laws through two key agencies: the Civil Rights Center and the Office of Federal Contract Compliance Programs. These agencies work to ensure compliance with EEO regulations in various employment settings.

"Equal Employment Opportunity." Web log. *U.S. Department of Labor* (blog), n.d. https://www.dol.gov/general/topic/discrimination.

10. EEOC — Chapter 4: Pushed Out, Burnt Out, or Sell Out

The Equal Employment Opportunity Commission (EEOC) is an independent federal agency responsible for promoting equal employment opportunities. It enforces federal civil rights laws, providing education and technical assistance, and offering support to applicants and employees of private employers, state and local governments, educational institutions, employment agencies, and labor organizations.

"Equal Employment Opportunity." Web log. *U.S. Department of Labor* (blog), n.d. https://www.dol.gov/general/topic/discrimination.

11. "Constructive termination" or "constructive discharge" — Chapter 2: Allies and Friends

"In general, the term "constructive discharge" is when a worker's resignation or retirement may be found not to be voluntary because the employer has created a hostile or intolerable work environment or has applied other forms of pressure or coercion which forced the employee to quit or resign. This often arises when an employer makes significant and severe changes in the terms and conditions of a worker's employment. What constitutes a constructive discharge is usually defined in state law and varies from state to state."

"WARN Advisor - Constructive Discharge." eLaws Advisors, n. d. https://webapps.dol.gov/elaws/eta/warn/glossary.asp?p=Constructive+Discharge.

12. "Soror" — Chapter 4: Pushed Out, Burnt Out, or Sell Out

Sorority sister in Delta Sigma Theta Sorority Incorporated of the Divine Nine

13. Dear Colleague Letter 2011 — Chapter 5: Grief and Loss

The 2011 "Dear Colleagues" letter from the U.S. Department of Education explains how schools must handle sexual violence and harassment under Title IX. It requires schools to have fair and quick procedures for dealing with complaints, use a standard that it's more likely than not that misconduct happened, offer temporary help to protect victims, and provide training to prevent these issues. The letter stresses that schools must act quickly to keep students safe and ensure they can continue their education without fear.

U.S. Department of Education, Office for Civil Rights. (2011, April 4). Dear Colleague Letter: Sexual Violence. https://www2.ed.gov/about/offices/list/ocr/letters/colleague-201104.html.

Part 2: Reflections Street

14. Reconstruction — Chapter 6: Insecurity Breeds Oppression

Presidential and Congressional Reconstruction began with President Andrew Johnson's approach, which aimed to quickly reunify the country without significant changes to the Southern way of life. This lenient strategy allowed many former Confederate leaders to regain power, restricting the rights of newly freed African Americans. However, Congressional Reconstruction, led by Radical Republicans, sought more substantial reforms. The Reconstruction Acts were passed, dividing the South into military districts to enforce civil rights and ensure that new state governments included protections for African American suffrage.

Three major amendments were added to the Constitution. The 13th Amendment, adopted in 1865, was supposed to abolish slavery in the United States. The 14th Amendment, ratified in 1868, granted citizenship to everyone born or naturalized in the U.S., including former slaves, and ensured equal protection under the law. The 15th Amendment, ratified in 1870, guaranteed that no one could be denied the right to vote based on race, color, or previous condition of servitude. These amendments aimed to secure the rights of African Americans and integrate them as equal citizens.

Congress established the Freedmen's Bureau in 1865 to help former slaves and poor whites in the South. This federal agency provided crucial services such as food, housing, medical care, and education. It was instrumental in helping former slaves transition to freedom by setting up schools, assisting with labor contracts, and legalizing marriages. Despite facing opposition and limited funding, the Freedmen's Bureau made significant contributions to improving the lives of many African Americans during the early Reconstruction years.

The Military Reconstruction Acts of 1867 were laws passed by Congress to enforce Reconstruction in the South. These acts divided the former Confederate states into five military districts, each led by a Union general. The goal was to maintain order and ensure new state constitutions included rights for African American men to vote. These military governments protected the civil rights of freedmen and facilitated their involvement in the political process. Federal troops' presence helped enforce these laws and prevent violence and intimidation against African Americans.

Despite the progress made during Reconstruction, many Southern whites resisted fiercely. This resistance led to the rise of white supremacist groups like the Ku Klux Klan, which used violence and terror to undermine Reconstruction efforts and maintain racial hierarchies. These groups targeted African Americans and their allies with lynchings, beatings, and arson. This backlash significantly hindered the enforcement of Reconstruction policies and created a climate of fear that weakened the protections and advancements made for African Americans during this period. The Reconstruction ended with the Compromise of 1877, which settled the disputed 1876 presidential election between Rutherford B. Hayes and Samuel J. Tilden.

As part of the compromise, Democrats accepted Hayes as president in exchange for the withdrawal of federal troops from the South. This marked the end of federal enforcement of Reconstruction policies, leading to the rise of "Redeemer" governments in the Southern states. These governments quickly enacted Jim Crow laws, instituting racial segregation and disenfranchising African Americans, effectively reversing many of the gains made during Reconstruction and initiating a long period of racial discrimination and inequality.

PBS. (n.d.). Reconstruction timeline. American Experience. https://www.pbs.org/wgbh/americanexperience/features/reconstruction-timeline/.

15. Lynch mobs during the Reconstruction Era — Chapter 6: Insecurity Breeds Oppression

Lynching is the act of killing someone, typically by hanging, carried out by a mob without a legal trial, often as a form of punishment or intimidation. During the Reconstruction Era, lynching mobs were groups of white supremacists who engaged in extrajudicial violence against African Americans and their allies. Operating outside the law, these mobs used lynching as a tool to instill fear, suppress civil rights, and maintain racial hierarchies. Their actions were meant to intimidate African Americans from exercising their newfound freedoms, such as voting or running for office, and to violently resist the social and political changes aimed at promoting equality. Despite some federal efforts to protect African Americans, local authorities often ignored these acts of violence, allowing lynching mobs to act with impunity and contributing to the eventual collapse of Reconstruction reforms.

During Reconstruction, the federal government made attempts to combat lynching and protect African Americans, including deploying federal troops and passing laws like the Enforcement Acts. However, these measures were often inadequate, as local authorities frequently ignored the violence, allowing lynching mobs to act with impunity. This widespread violence played a significant role in the collapse of Reconstruction and led to the establishment of Jim Crow laws, which enforced racial segregation and disenfranchisement in the South.

Koulish, R., Slocum, L. A., Welsh, B. C., & Zane, S. N. (2016). The effects of immigration enforcement policies on Latino immigrant perceptions of law enforcement: An exploratory analysis. Sociological Science, 3, 860-888. https://sociologicalscience.com/download/vol-3/september/SocSci_v3_860to888.pdf.

Smith, A. (2021). Integrating technology in the classroom: Best practices and pedagogical strategies. Learning and Leading with Technology, 15(3), Article 5. https://ecommons.udayton.edu/cgi/viewcontent.cgi?article=1270&context=lxl

16. Jim Crow laws and Segregation — Chapter 6: Insecurity Breeds Oppression

Jim Crow laws were state and local regulations in the Southern United States, enforced from the late 1800s to the mid-1900s, that mandated racial segregation and aimed to disenfranchise African Americans. These laws required the separation of races in public facilities and services, including schools, transportation, restrooms, and restaurants, under the guise of "separate but equal." In reality, the facilities and services for African Americans were vastly inferior and poorly funded compared to those for whites. Jim Crow laws entrenched economic, educational, and social disadvantages for African Americans, supported by the U.S. Supreme Court's 1896 Plessy v. Ferguson decision, which remained in effect until the Civil Rights Movement of the 1960s brought about significant legal and societal changes.

Segregation is the practice of separating people into different groups based on characteristics like race, ethnicity, or religion. This separation can be enforced by laws (de jure segregation) or arise from social norms and practices (de facto segregation). Segregation occurs in various areas of life, such as education, housing, transportation, and employment, often leading to unequal opportunities and treatment for the affected groups. The intent and effect of segregation are typically to maintain social and economic disparities between different groups.

Vogler, R. C. (2023). Jim Crow laws. Lucent Press. https://www.google.com/books/edition/Jim_Crow_Laws/yIb-DEAAAQBAJ?hl=en&gbpv=1&dq=what+are+the+jim+crow+laws&pg=PP1&cover.

Green, R. P. (1988). The paradox of the U.S. Supreme Court's retroactivity doctrine. Minnesota Law Review, 73(5), 1201-1252. https://scholarship.law.umn.edu/cgi/viewcontent.cgi?article=3709&context=mlr.

17. Do Better by Rachel Ricketts — Chapter 8: Why Don't White Men Bother Me as Much?

Rachel Ricketts is a racial justice educator, spiritual activist, and speaker who addresses the intersection of racial justice and spirituality. Based in Vancouver, she uses her platform to challenge systemic racism and advocate for marginalized communities, integrating spiritual practices to promote both internal and external transformation. Her book, Do Better: Spiritual Activism for Fighting and Healing from White Supremacy, combines her personal stories with actionable advice on combating white supremacy. It urges readers, particularly white individuals, to face discomfort as part of their anti-racist journey, emphasizing a holistic approach that includes spiritual activism to heal from racial trauma and achieve collective liberation.

McGonegal, Julie. "Rachel Ricketts on Spirituality's Essential Place in Activism." Web log. *Broadview* (blog), May 7, 2021. https://broadview.org/rachel-ricketts-interview/.

Ricketts, R. (n.d.). Rachel Ricketts: Spiritual Activist, Racial Justice Educator, Public Speaker. Retrieved May 17, 2024, from https://www.rachelricketts.com/.

18. Employee Resource Groups — Chapter 9: ERGs

Employee Resource Groups (ERGs) are voluntary, employee-led groups formed based on shared characteristics or life experiences, aiming to foster a diverse and inclusive workplace. They support professional development, enhance employee engagement and retention, influence company policies, and drive innovation by providing a platform for diverse perspectives. ERGs also assist in recruitment, improve community engagement, and contribute to corporate social responsibility efforts, making them vital for creating a supportive and innovative work environment.

Indeed Editorial Team. (n.d.). Employee Resource Groups: Your complete guide. Indeed. Retrieved June 9, 2024, from https://www.indeed.com/hire/c/info/employee-resource-groups?gad_source=1&psafe_param=1&gclid=Cj0KCQjwpZWzBhC0ARIsACvjWROeRS27LYKShf9fQRkpMPPVqM5idDBkl-A-MITu76T5ajOpsqQwaEAaAoMfEALw_wcB&aceid=&gclsrc=aw.dsm.

19. DSM (Diagnostic Statistical Manual) — Chapter 10: $125,000

The Diagnostic and Statistical Manual of Mental Disorders, Fifth Edition, Text Revision (DSM-5-TR) is a key reference developed with input from over 200 experts, reflecting the latest scientific research. It introduces new diagnoses such as prolonged grief disorder, updates criteria for over 70 disorders, and incorporates ICD-10-CM codes for suicidal and non-suicidal self-injury. Additionally, it addresses the impact of racism and discrimination on mental health. This manual aids clinicians and researchers in enhancing the diagnosis, treatment, and study of mental disorders.

Cleveland Clinic. (n.d.). Diagnostic and Statistical Manual (DSM-5). Cleveland Clinic. Retrieved June 9, 2024, from https://my.clevelandclinic.org/health/articles/24291-diagnostic-and-statistical-manual-dsm-5

American Psychiatric Association. (n.d.). Diagnostic and Statistical Manual of Mental Disorders (DSM). American Psychiatric Association. Retrieved June 9, 2024, from https://www.psychiatry.org/psychiatrists/practice/dsm.

Part 3: Rehab Drive

20. Sifted as wheat (Scripture verse) — Chapter 11: Control

"And the Lord said, Simon, Simon, behold, Satan hath desired to have you, that he may sift you as wheat." — Luke 22:31, NKJV

Jesus tells Simon (Peter) that Satan wants to test his faith severely, just as wheat is sifted to separate it from the chaff. He emphasizes the intensity of the spiritual trial Peter is about to face. The passage where Jesus warns Peter that Satan wants to sift him like wheat signifies the various challenges and tests individuals may face. It highlights how one's faith, beliefs, and resilience can be severely tested through difficult situations. The message underscores the importance of being prepared for such trials and remaining steadfast in one's principles and convictions during tough times.

Bible Gateway. (n.d.). Luke 22:31-34 (King James Version). Retrieved June 9, 2024, from https://www.biblegateway.com/passage/?search=Luke%2022%3A31-34&version=KJV.

21. Harriet Tubman — Chapter 12: The Niggers I've Seen Sold

Harriet Tubman was an African American abolitionist and political activist born into slavery around 1822. She is best known for her role as a "conductor" on the Underground Railroad, where she led numerous enslaved people to freedom. Tubman also served as a spy and nurse for the Union Army during the Civil War. Her efforts were crucial in the fight against slavery, and she is celebrated for her bravery and commitment to justice and equality.

National Women's History Museum. (n.d.). Harriet Tubman. Retrieved June 9, 2024, from https://www.womenshistory.org/education-resources/biographies/harriet-tubman.

National Park Service. (n.d.). Harriet Tubman. Retrieved June 9, 2024, from https://www.nps.gov/people/harriet-tubman.htm.

Part 4: Recovery Circle

22. "Still I Rise" by Maya Angelou — Chapter 22: Violent White Women

"Still I Rise" by Maya Angelou is an inspiring poem about resilience and overcoming oppression. It highlights the strength and dignity of marginalized individuals, especially Black women, who face adversity and discrimination with confidence and self-respect. The recurring line "I rise" signifies an indomitable spirit and the resolve to overcome challenges. Angelou's poem asserts independence and self-worth, motivating readers to stand strong and persevere.

"You may write me down in history
With your bitter, twisted lies,
You may trod me in the very dirt
But still, like dust, I'll rise.
Does my sassiness upset you?
Why are you beset with gloom?
'Cause I walk like I've got oil wells
Pumping in my living room.
Just like moons and like suns,
With the certainty of tides,
Just like hopes springing high,
Still I'll rise.
Did you want to see me broken?
Bowed head and lowered eyes?
Shoulders falling down like teardrops,
Weakened by my soulful cries?
Does my haughtiness offend you?
Don't you take it awful hard
'Cause I laugh like I've got gold mines
Diggin' in my own backyard.
You may shoot me with your words,
You may cut me with your eyes,

You may kill me with your hatefulness,
But still, like air, I'll rise.
Does my sexiness upset you?
Does it come as a surprise
That I dance like I've got diamonds
At the meeting of my thighs?
Out of the huts of history's shame
I rise
Up from a past that's rooted in pain
I rise
I'm a black ocean, leaping and wide,
Welling and swelling I bear in the tide.
Leaving behind nights of terror and fear
I rise
Into a daybreak that's wondrously clear
I rise
Bringing the gifts that my ancestors gave,
I am the dream and the hope of the slave.
I rise
I rise
I rise."

M. (1978). "Still I rise". Academy of American Poets. Retrieved from Poets.org.

Part 5: Runteldat Way

23. Restorative Circle — Chapter 26: The Big Wins That Meant Nothing

A restorative circle is a structured dialogue used in classrooms and other settings to build relationships, foster community, and develop conflict resolution skills. Participants sit in a circle to promote equality and share their thoughts and feelings, typically led by a facilitator and guided by agreed-upon norms. This practice proactively addresses conflicts, enhances communication, and supports social and emotional learning, effectively reducing school violence and absenteeism through understanding and collaboration.

Neforos, M. C. (2023, September). Restorative circles: A platform for student voice. American School Counselor Association. Retrieved from https://www.schoolcounselor.org/Newsletters/September-2023/Restorative-Circles-A-Platform-for-Student-Voice.

24. CYA — Chapter 27: "The Budget"

"CYA" stands for "Cover Your Ass." It is a colloquial term that describes actions taken to protect oneself from blame, criticism, or legal liability, often in professional or bureaucratic contexts. This typically involves creating a record of decisions, following protocols, and documenting communications to ensure accountability and prevent future repercussions.

25. Summary of the story of Baal and Elijah — Chapter 28: "Baal-or" University

The story of Baal and Elijah, from the biblical book of 1 Kings, tells of the prophet Elijah confronting King Ahab of Israel and his promotion of the Canaanite god Baal. Elijah predicts a drought as punishment for the nation's idolatry, and after three years, challenges the prophets of Baal to a test on Mount Carmel to prove whose god is real. Yahweh, the God of Israel, answers Elijah's prayer with fire that consumes his sacrifice, demonstrating Yahweh's power. Today, the story resonates as a reminder of the clash between faith in God and the allure of idolatry or false beliefs.

It underscores the importance of steadfast faith and the power of divine intervention in the face of adversity or societal pressures.

"The Church of Jesus Christ of Latter-day Saints. 'Elijah and the Priests of Baal.' "Old Testament Stories, 2022". Accessed June 16, 2024. https://www.churchofjesuschrist.org/study/manual/old-testament-stories-2022/elijah-and-the-priests-of-baal?lang=eng.

Bible Gateway. '1 Kings 18:20-40 (English Standard Version).' Accessed June 16, 2024. https://www.biblegateway.com/passage/?search=1%20Kings%2018%3A20-40&version=ESV.

26. Harriet Tubman and the cost of going back to free others — Chapter 30: To Sue or Not to Sue

Harriet Tubman, an iconic figure in American history, not only escaped slavery herself but also dedicated her life to rescuing others through the Underground Railroad. After gaining her freedom in 1849, Tubman made numerous perilous journeys back into slave-holding states, risking capture, injury, or death to guide enslaved individuals to freedom in the Northern states and Canada.

These missions were incredibly dangerous. Tubman had to navigate through unfamiliar territory, avoid patrols and slave catchers, and endure harsh weather conditions while ensuring the safety of her passengers. Despite the dangers, Tubman was relentless in her pursuit of freedom for others, earning her the nickname "Moses" for leading her people out of bondage. Her commitment to the cause of abolition and her willingness to face danger head-on make Harriet Tubman a symbol of courage, resilience, and selflessness in the fight against slavery. Harriet Tubman, renowned for her courageous efforts in the Underground Railroad, exemplifies extraordinary bravery and selflessness. She repeatedly risked her life to lead enslaved individuals to freedom, making an estimated 13 missions and freeing approximately 70 people. Tubman's bravery was most evident in her decision to return to the South repeatedly, despite the danger, to lead others to freedom.

National Park Service. "Harriet Tubman Underground Railroad National Historical Park: Myths vs. Facts." Accessed June 16, 2024. https://www.nps.gov/hatu/planyourvisit/upload/md_tubmanfactsheet_mythsfacts_2.pdf.

27. "Creamy Crack" — Chapter 32: When I Knew It Was Over

"Creamy crack" is a colloquial term used in the African American community to refer to hair relaxers or chemical straighteners. These products are used to chemically alter the texture of curly or kinky hair to make it straighter and easier to manage. The term "creamy crack" humorously plays on the addictive nature of hair relaxers, as once someone starts using them, they may feel dependent on them to maintain a certain hairstyle or appearance.

Hunter-Gadsden, K. (2022, June 16). As more Black women wean off of the creamy crack, experts weigh in on the natural hair movement. *The Root*. Retrieved June 16, 2024, from https://www.theroot.com/as-more-black-women-wean-off-of-the-creamy-crack-expert-1849748198

28. Luke 12:2-3

"What is done in the dark WILL come to light"

This verse urges people to live righteously because, eventually, what is said and done will come to be revealed. Truth triumphs falsehood. It considers accountability, righteousness, and ethics.

29. Luke 23:34

"And Jesus said, 'Father, forgive them, for they know not what they do.' And they cast lots to divide his garments."

30. Ecclesiastes 3:1-8

"To every thing there is a season, and a time to every purpose under the heaven:

2 A time to be born, and a time to die; a time to plant, and a time to pluck up that which is planted;

3 A time to kill, and a time to heal; a time to break down, and a time to build up;

4 A time to weep, and a time to laugh; a time to mourn, and a time to dance;

5 A time to cast away stones, and a time to gather stones together; a time to embrace, and a time to refrain from embracing;

6 A time to get, and a time to lose; a time to keep, and a time to cast away;

7 A time to rend, and a time to sew; a time to keep silence, and a time to speak;

8 A time to love, and a time to hate; a time of war, and a time of peace."

Life is composed of various seasons and moments, each with its appropriate time. It lists pairs of contrasting activities—such as birth and death, mourning and dancing—to illustrate that every action and emotion has its rightful place in the human experience. The message underscores the balance of life's different phases, suggesting that understanding this balance can help us navigate our lives more gracefully.

Bible Gateway. (n.d.). Ecclesiastes 3:1-8 (King James Version). Retrieved June 9, 2024, from https://www.biblegateway.com/passage/?search=Ecclesiastes%203%3A1-8&version=KJV.

Receipts

BFSA Steering Committee

BRITTNEY WARDLAW, J.D.

Disciplinary Action Notice (2017)

Employee Disciplinary Action Notice

Employee Information

Employee Name:	Britney Wardlaw	Date:	May 31, 2017
Employee ID:	892450376	Job Title:	Deputy Title IX Coordinator
Manager:	Kristan Tucker	Department:	Title IX Office

Type of Warning

☒ First Level Warning   ☐ Second Level Warning   ☐ Final Warning

Description of Concern

This Disciplinary Action Notice is to inform you of significant deficiencies and concerning behaviors regarding your performance as Deputy Title IX Coordinator. We have discussed on numerous occasions the need for immediate improvement in a number of areas for which you are responsible. These discussions include the following:

4/19/17 – we verbally discussed performance expectations, the importance of completion of tasks and being responsive, as well as the need for your leadership presence in the office

4/21/17 – we discussed areas of disappointment including work items not being completed, the need for you to catch up on your knowledge of OCR guidance, regulatory items, policy, and procedures; I also expressed concern about how your knowledge and application of these items is critical to serving our students (there was an acknowledgement during this meeting of short-comings as well as how behind your former employer was)

5/5/17 – we discussed the tasks that were given to you on Monday, May 1st which included contacting panel members and scheduling locations, I expressed my disappointment and concern because this was still not completed, unfortunately this affected the Consortium schedule and we talked through my concern related to a lack of prioritization and meeting deadlines

5/6/17 through 5/7/17 – our office received a report and I was unable to reach you after trying multiple times throughout the weekend, on Sunday we when we were able to connect. We previously discussed the importance of being available and responsive by checking email and phone at least once a day over weekends.

5/15/17 – we discussed a list of cases which needed to be closed by the next day, these cases should have been closed previously, in addition, the hearing panel process was still not completed and we discussed the need to finalize this as soon as possible

5/22/17 – I identified that the panel members had not yet received the information related to the upcoming hearing, your response was that needed to still be completed, however, we discussed this happening much sooner since the hearing was 2 days away

5/24/17 – it was my understanding that you had instructed our staff to walk individuals outside, we discussed that this was not appropriate and would have placed members of the team in uncertain situations which could have a detrimental effect on their safety, in addition I also informed you that I

was aware that you had asked an administrative staff member about a policy interpretation concern. This is out of the scope of the administrative role and lies within your role as the deputy. We also discussed your gaps of knowledge related to Clery compliance and common best practices, during this conversation you stated "I feel like I can't do anything right here"

5/26/17 – I mentioned to you that we still have over 30 students who have not been contacted according to our policy. You acknowledged this had not been completed as well. As of 8am on May 30th, this task had not yet been addressed.

In addition to these conversations, we have also discussed the critical situation the Title IX office is in, in terms of volume of work and the need for timeliness, the intense internal and external focus on this office and its processes and the importance of our work as mission critical to Baylor at this time and how successful execution of your role is necessary to alleviate these burdens. These deficiencies have, in turn, prevented me from handing off to you the full spectrum of duties assigned to the Deputy Coordinator position, which is concerning as the volume and intensity of work will increase in August as the full student body returns to campus. Because your performance has been below expectations for the level of responsibility associated with your position, improvements will be required in order to continue as an employee in good standing. You are being placed on a First Level Warning with this Performance Improvement Plan for 30 days. An immediate improvement of your performance is expected and interim evaluations will take place on a weekly basis to assess your progress. After no later than 30 days of working within this plan, a final evaluation will take place to determine next steps. Please be aware that failure to meet performance expectations of this position could result in further disciplinary action up to and including separation of employment.

It is our hope that this feedback will be received constructively and that the required adjustments are made to meet these expectations. <u>Our goal is to retain you as a fully contributing member of the Title IX staff, and we encourage you to bring to our attention any concerns that may prevent you from meeting these expectations.</u>

The areas of concern include the following:

- Using technical knowledge to complete assignments and tasks at an expert level.
- Having accountability for results within assignments.
- Creating a leadership presence within assignments and administrative services.
- Having expert knowledge of assignments area.
- Meeting deadlines and effectively managing projects.
- The ability to communicate effectively, including presenting ideas to others.
- Engaging in critical thinking and logical reasoning at an expert level.
- Understanding how to be an effective member of the Title IX team as well as understanding your role within the team.
- Willingness to take direction from the Title IX Coordinator.
- Inability to prioritize tasks and assignments to ensure the most important items are addressed and completed as soon as possible.

Required Plan for Improvement

The following plan for improvement details the current and ongoing expectations required for the role of the Deputy Title IX Coordinator as well as specific actionable items:

Performance Expectations

- **Accountability for Results.** Make realistic commitments for accomplishing tasks, by balancing the quality of work with meeting deadlines. Demonstrate ability to effectively complete tasks even when obstacles arise.
- **Attention to Detail.** Check work to ensure accuracy and completeness. Compare observations or finished work to what is expected to find inconsistencies. Remain aware and take care of details that are easy to overlook or dismiss as insignificant.
- **Analytical and Reasoning.** Identify key facts in a range of data and notice when data appears incorrect or incomplete. Distinguish information that is not pertinent to a decision or solution and present concise summaries of said information/data. Prepare statistical reports on number, nature, and deposition of complaints in order to identify patterns or trends and make recommendations. Additionally, when working with the investigators in evaluating the thoroughness of an investigation and developing the rationale analysis of a preliminary investigative report, utilize analytical and logical thought process to ensure a detailed rationale is provided.
- **Decision-making and Judgment.** Decision-making should be based on current University policies, procedures, and best practices within the area of Title IX and VAWA. Consider lessons learned from your and others past experiences, the University climate, and the impact of the decisions on others and the broader campus community. Prioritizing and triaging tasks as they are assigned is critical to the effectiveness of this office and serving our campus community.
- **Strategic Vision and Process.** Develop and implement case management plan for each reported Title IX incident processing safety concerns, necessary interim measures, jurisdiction, and determining next steps. Meet with complainants to provide rights, resources, and options. Follow up with complainants and/or initial reporters in a timely manner. Regularly monitor and utilize operational procedures to ensure an efficient and effective response to complaints.
- **Stay up to date on subject area.** Keep updated on shifts and best practices in the areas of sexual and gender-based harassment, due process, trauma informed investigative techniques, intimate partner violence, sexual violence, and stalking by being up to date on case law, OCR resolution agreements, federal and state guidance, regulations, and/or laws.
- **Compliance and Collaboration.** Based on the updates and best practices, collaborate and consult with supervisor to continuously identify and integrate best practices in the Title IX investigation and case management process as well as implement improvements. Audit processes and policies with the Title IX Coordinator and other campus offices (such as the Title IX policy, first reports, interviewing techniques, investigative processes, hearings, etc) to ensure compliance. Be proactive in searching templates, case files, protocols, and the policy rather than seeking a quick response from other team members.
- **Keep your supervisor informed.** It is better for your supervisor to hear information from you than from someone else. It is wise for you to notify (either by email or verbally) your supervisor pertaining to conversations with anyone outside of the department related to concerns or issues. Furthermore, your supervisor should be informed of communication occurring with anyone at your supervisor's level and above or who is a significant decision maker within the

University (such as legal counsel, police department, student life, judicial affairs, counseling center, human resources, EC, and/or the provost office).
- **Leadership Presence.** Lead by consistent examples. Clearly communicate expectations. Convey confidence in the ability to prevail over challenges to reach goals. It is important to link mission, vision, values, goals, and strategies to everyday work. In the absence of the Title IX Coordinator, assume Title IX Coordinator duties as appropriate and necessary regarding critical decisions. Understand that each member of the team plays a valuable role in the processing of cases, and while a hierarchy must exist in order to effectively manage any organization, recognizing the input of each team member as critical to the process.
- **Presenting to the campus community.** When presenting ideas, interact with the audience, read body language, gather feedback, and hold their attention. When listeners fail to grasp concepts, it is critical to take steps to ensure comprehension. Also, come prepared; gauge the audience's level of knowledge by tailoring the presentation to the audience. Anticipate what questions will be asked and prepare answers accordingly.

Action Items
1. **Meet deadlines.** Work diligently to complete all tasks assigned to you within the provided deadline. We have discussed that there are 30 to 40 cases currently not being addressed. It is imperative that these cases be addressed in the appropriate manner according to our Title IX Policy and procedures. Provide a weekly report on back logged cases and progress.
2. **Work more proactively.** Think through upcoming deadlines and tasks that need to be completed. Seek to troubleshoot issues before they become a problem. This includes communicating materials to the hearing panel at least 7 calendars days prior to the hearing as well as informing me via email when an obstacle surfaces which could prevent any deadline being met.
3. **Strengthen professional credibility.** Research answers to find correct information rather than providing a "best guess." When utilizing feedback provided by others, give credit to that individual's contribution to the decision you reached as well as explain your thought process. When situations surface that need my guidance following these guidelines: Summarize the situation in 3 to 5 sentences; provide 2 options with thought through rationales, identify a recommendation from the 2 options along with the reasoning why it was selected. This can be provided in person or by email.
4. **Open and respectful communication with supervisor.** Keep your supervisor informed of important issues that arise in a respectful manner. Scheduled weekly one on one meetings with me. In preparation for those meetings, provide an agenda with priority matters identified. In the event we are unable to meet face to face, an email is required to summarize the week.
5. **Basic management of case files, new reports, and processes/procedures.** It is critical for the University as well as those we serve (students, faculty, and staff) to be diligent in our work and to address issues brought to our attention in a timely and efficient way. Due to the lack of baseline knowledge, I have made arrangements for a consultant to provide additional training in the areas of processes and procedures. The details regarding this are still in process. This one on one specialized training will be mandatory and the timing will be contingent upon the consultant's availability. Once this training is complete, it is

expected for you to demonstrate an understanding for the material by implement it in your work going forward.

In addition to the plan for improvement, I would like to remind you that all employees and their dependents have access to an employee assistance plan (EAP). The EAP is available 24/7 at (888) 628-4844 or www.guidanceresources.com.

Consequences of Repeat Concerns:

In summary, the goal of this disciplinary action notice is to ensure Britney is aware of the above mentioned concerns and makes the appropriate improvements required to be a contributing member of the Title IX team. Continuation of the outlined concerns of poor performance, instances or concerns of misconduct, and/or other policy violations may result in further disciplinary action up to and including termination from employment.

Acknowledgment of Receipt of Notice

By signing this form, you confirm that you understand the information in this warning. You also confirm that you and your manager have discussed the warning and a plan for improvement. Signing this form does not necessarily indicate that you agree with this warning.

_____ _____
Employee Signature   Date

_____ _____
Manager Signature   Date

_____ _____
Human Resources Consultant   Date

Performance Evaluation (2019)

PERFORMANCE FEEDBACK 2019

The purpose of this form is to provide a documented summary of the performance feedback conversations between managers and employees to support professional development. For employees and managers, the process offers a time to recognize accomplishments, learn from experience, identify and develop strengths and areas of improvement in performance, discuss the previous year's goals, and plan for goals for the coming year. In addition, the content is used to inform performance-related areas for the University, such as professional development needs and merit-based compensation allocation.

Employee Identification

Name: Brittney Wardlaw   **Division:** N/A

Job Title: Manager of Equity and Civil Rights   **Department:** Equity Office

Hire Date: 1/30/17   **Employee ID:** 892450376

PART ONE: The Past Year

Review goals from the past year and provide the contributions and challenges of the work for each.

Goals	Contributions & Challenges Related to Goal
Employee Response: **Title:** Intersectionality of Equity-related Policies Review of the Sexual and Gender-Based Harassment Policy, the Civil Rights Policy & Procedures for Employees and the Civil Rights Policy & Procedures for Students for ways in which they connect, overlap, and influence one another. Also, exam how these policies, practices, and structures operate with factors such as race, gender, disabilities, etc. to leverage access to learning opportunities. Continue to look for ways to implement practices that are responsive and relevant to faculty, staff, and students' allegations of harassment, discrimination, etc.	Yes, achieved. 1) I was able to review policy as a result of the receipt of overlapping reports, as well as a collaborative review with Shiri Brown to identify areas of improvement. 2) Created an additional bias training in hopes of educating staff, faculty, and students as it relates to their interactions with colleagues. 3) Outlined, and created a proposal for formulating a stronger and more detailed alternative resolution arm for resolve of equity related issues.
Title: Intersectionality of Equity-related Policies Review of the Sexual and Gender-Based Harassment Policy, the Civil Rights Policy & Procedures for Employees and the Civil Rights Policy & Procedures for Students for ways in which they connect, overlap, and influence one another. Also, exam how these policies, practices, and structures operate with factors such as race, gender, disabilities, etc. to leverage access to learning opportunities. Continue to look for ways to implement practices that are responsive and relevant to faculty, staff, and students' allegations of harassment, discrimination, etc.	
Due:	**Completed:**
	Status:
Goals	Contributions & Challenges Related to Goal

https://global.hgncloud.com/baylor/welcome.jsp?selectedtab=PERFORMANC&selectedsubtab=evaluations

BRITTNEY WARDLAW, J.D.

4/23/2020   Saba TalentSpace

Employee **Title:** Affirmative Action Compliance
Response: Gather a better understanding on specific Affirmative Action requirements - Executive Order 11246, Vietnam Era Veterans' Readjustment Assistance Act of 1974, as amended (VEVRAA), Section 503 of the Rehabilitation Act of 1973, as amended, and Executive Order 13496

This was partially achieved. My title and responsibilities changed in June 2018. My primary responsibilities no longer required the expertise I sought originally sought as it relates to AA. However, I attended several workshops at the AAAED National conference on AA. I also participated in a Listen Session with the OFCCP in Washington DC with several representatives of higher education across the nation.

Title: Affirmative Action Compliance
Gather a better understanding on specific Affirmative Action requirements - Executive Order 11246, Vietnam Era Veterans' Readjustment Assistance Act of 1974, as amended (VEVRAA), Section 503 of the Rehabilitation Act of 1973, as amended, and Executive Order 13496

Due:

Completed:

Status:

Goals	Contributions & Challenges Related to Goal

Employee **Title:** Professional Development
Response: Attend and participate in professional development conferences/workshops to build strengths and close development gaps; i.e., NILG, OFCCP conferences/webinars, AAAED, etc.

Yes, achieved. Attended the AAAED National Conference. I was also accepted and participated in the New Professionals Academy (NPA) with AAAED. Additionally, I submitted a proposal that was accepted to be presented at the next AAAED national conference. I also gained membership with SHRM. Participated in several webinars, lunch & learns, & workshops. Including but not limited to "Giving and Receiving Feedback as a Minority," "Being a POC at a faith-based PWI," and "Race Equity Institute Follow-Up."

Title: Professional Development
Attend and participate in professional development conferences/workshops to build strengths and close development gaps; i.e., NILG, OFCCP conferences/webinars, AAAED, etc.

Due:

Completed:

Status:

Additional Goals & Information (optional):

Provide a description of major contributions and challenges not addressed in the goals from the past year, as well as any other comments you would like to include.

Employee Response: I created an outline for implementation of Restorative Practices at Baylor. Additionally, I went through a 40hr Basic Mediation Certification in order to obtain additional training and expertise for implementation.

I had the privilege of representing Baylor University as United Way (UW) Co-Chair and successfully raised $89K. I've been asked to participate on the UW Safety Net Investment Council for the next two years. In addition, I am a member of both the Steering Committee and the Executive Board for the newly formulated Black Faculty & Staff Association as President-Elect. I am also an active participant on both the Diversity Council, as well as the Executive Diversity Council.

Despite taking maternity leave, I was able to make significant traction in the development of the Equity Office as it relates to alternative resolution as outlined in the Civil Rights Policies & Title IX Policy.

Brittney has taken the lead on many important projects. I appreciate her exploring Restorative Practices. It is great that she gained the certification in Mediation. I appreciate her leadership with United Way and the Black Faculty and Staff Association. I support all that she is doing in these various areas.

Feedback on Past Year

This section focuses on the past year, both *what* work was done and the *way* in which it was accomplished. Feedback is provided for Overall Skills & Performance and each of the Core Commitments using the options listed below. In addition, comments may be included for each Commitment to provide examples and clarification.

FEEDBACK OPTIONS

Area of Mastery

Performance exceeds expectations for position both in work and impact. Uses strengths in area to benefit the University. Is a clear role model and/or mentor in helping others develop this commitment. *Requires comment.

Area of Competence

Performance is steady, reliable and is maintained with a minimum of supervision. Is reliably and consistently successful using this commitment. Demonstrates ability to integrate a wide variety of skills to effectively solve problems and carry out duties, responsibilities, and objectives. Reflects values of organization in this area.

Area of Needed Development

Needs further development, guidance and/or evaluation to demonstrate this commitment consistently at a level appropriate for the position. Performance approaches acceptable standards for position and extra effort is needed to improve or continue improvement. Working toward gaining proficiency. Achieves some but not all goals and is willing to acquire necessary knowledge and skills.

Area of Concern

Regularly demonstrates behaviors inconsistent with this commitment. Performance is below standard of position and improvement is required. Primary responsibilities are not being met and important objectives have not been accomplished. *Requires comment.

PERFORMANCE FEEDBACK TOOLS

The following tools are provided to support a productive and effective feedback conversation.

Performance Matrix

The performance matrix provides further description of each Core Commitment and behavioral examples. It serves as a useful reference when determining the feedback option selection for each Core Commitment. The performance matrix can be found HERE.

Writing Comments

For each Commitment, it is helpful to provide examples to illustrate the feedback rating chosen. Information on writing positive and development feedback can be found HERE

BRITTNEY WARDLAW, J.D.

4/23/2020 Saba TalentSpace

CORE COMMITMENTS

Commitment	Feedback Selection	Comments:
	Employee Area of Competence	
Account for Stewardship of Time, Resources, & Self Discernment Deliver Results Plan & Organize	Area of Competence	
	Employee Area of Mastery	I am an enthusiastic advocate for incorporating campus partners into the work. I have demonstrated the importance of working collaboratively through email communication, phone calls, and taking initiative to host meetings to encourage communication. When at all possible, I encourage the sharing of communication inter-department to get the best results.
Build Relationships & Work Collaboratively Relationship Management Respect Diversity Teamwork & Collaboration	Area of Mastery	Brittney builds relationships well with others across campus. She is great at collaborating and working as a team. She is very respectful of others. Campus partners find her trustworthy and know that they can reach out to her.
	Employee Area of Mastery	I have been sought out by numerous entities to represent the University in various capacities. Whether that has been in conjunction with our partnership with Waco (e.g. United Way), or as a representative of a reputable Faculty/Staff of color. I enthusiastically accept the responsibility to represent, educate, or whatever is required on behalf of the University. These opportunities include and go beyond my role as a Manager of Civil Rights & Equity, but ultimately the work is helpful in creating more equitable spaces across campus.
Commit to University/Departmental Mission & Vision Integrity Organizational/Dept. Commitment Organizational Compliance & Safety	Area of Mastery	She fully and enthusiastically supports the University mission. She whole heartedly strives for the best and keeps the University mission at the forefront. She has the utmost integrity. She is trustworthy and fully follows process and procedures.
	Employee Area of Mastery	Equity is already an area with unclear guidelines and direction. Therefore, the work requires creativity, and active problem solving, and adaptation regularly. Actively challenge the status quo and submit creative solutions for consideration.
Pursue Excellence through Continuous Improvement Adapt to Change Creativity & Innovation Problem-Solve Quality Focus	Area of Mastery	Brittney adapts well to change. She is willing to think creatively and find a solution. She focuses on high quality in each of her activities.

4/23/2020   Saba TalentSpace

	Employee	Area of Mastery	I have extensive prior experience in the area of restorative practices and alternative resolution. Working to creatively implement this prior experience in both the Equity and Title IX Offices. Often sought after by various areas such as Student Conduct, BRT, HR, and BFSA to offer insight and knowledge as it pertains to the Civil Rights, discrimination, harassment, diversity, inclusion, and I take advantage of any opportunities that I am made aware of to participate in (i.e. workshops, lectures) to sharpen my skills as it relates to education and inclusion for gender, race, ethnicity, etc.
Seek Learning & Apply Knowledge Continual Learning Professional Knowledge		Area of Mastery	Brittney is continually learning and applying new knowledge. She is eager and willing to learn new skills or professional knowledge. She seeks opportunities to expand her knowledge. I appreciate her willingness in this area.
	Employee	Area of Competence	
Serve Others Respectfully Communicate Effectively Constituent Service		Area of Competence	She serves others very well and is respectful of all that she interacts with. She communicates well with others. One area of development could include to communicate more often and respond to others in a timely manner, when possible. It would be helpful to me to update me with any possible crisis or explosive situations and not wait until the next scheduled meeting.
	Employee	Area of Competence	
Overall Skills & Performance Job Skills Work Performance		Area of Competence	Brittney performs her job and skills very well. She is dedicated to her work. She is effective in her role. One area for development would include timely responses or conclusions to investigations. Investigations often are complicated and involve various constituents across campus. She may need to follow up more with others in order to close out investigations in a timely manner.

PART TWO: The Future Year—GOALS

For each goal, include a title and description. The description may include: how the goal will affect the department, division, or University; the method by which the outcome will be measured; and the purpose of or reasoning for the goal. A due date may be entered as well. To add another goal, click on *Add New Goal*. The form can accommodate up to five goals. Information on goal-setting may be found HERE

Goals

Employee Response: Title: Formalize Alternative Resolution Options

With the recent receipt of certification in Basic Mediation and the impending re-education of Restorative Justice practices, I will use these skill sets to implement tangible opportunities to process complaints through an alternative resolution mechanism. We will educate the Baylor community of the practicality and functionality of restorative practices across campus. This will be in collaboration with Student Conduct and other areas of Student Life, BRT, and Human Resources. We will work to build an infrastructure that supports processing 100% more cases through more restorative means.

Title: Formalize Alternative Resolution Options

With the recent receipt of certification in Basic Mediation and the impending re-education of Restorative

4/23/2020

Justice practices, I will use these skill sets to implement tangible opportunities to process complaints through an alternative resolution mechanism. We will educate the Baylor community of the practicality and functionality of restorative practices across campus. This will be in collaboration with Student Conduct and other areas of Student Life, BRT, and Human Resources. We will work to build an infrastructure that supports processing 100% more cases through more restorative means.

Due:

Goals

Employee Response: Title: Bolster Education Curriculum
Add two additional trainings/workshops to be available to faculty, staff, and students to continue to educate Baylor to becoming a more equitable community. Additionally, coordinate with various departments and colleges on campus in order to organize and schedule presentations campus wide.

Title: Bolster Education Curriculum
Add two additional trainings/workshops to be available to faculty, staff, and students to continue to educate Baylor to becoming a more equitable community. Additionally, coordinate with various departments and colleges on campus in order to organize and schedule presentations campus wide.

Due:

Goals

Employee Response: Title: Build Campus Partnerships
The primary partnership growth and strength focus is with the Equity Office and Title IX. With the primary goal of implementation of restorative practices, I will work with Title IX and Equity create a process whereby the Baylor community can participate in an established restoration process. I will also work with various other departments and colleges to communicate the intent, goal, and purposes of our work, but also to be in relationship in preparation for collaboration.

Title: Build Campus Partnerships
The primary partnership growth and strength focus is with the Equity Office and Title IX. With the primary goal of implementation of restorative practices, I will work with Title IX and Equity create a process whereby the Baylor community can participate in an established restoration process. I will also work with various other departments and colleges to communicate the intent, goal, and purposes of our work, but also to be in relationship in preparation for collaboration.

Due:

PART THREE: Manager Comments

It has been great to work with Brittney this past year. I enjoy our time together. She is very effective in her role. She is trustworthy, has the utmost integrity, and treats others with respect. She is a leader in the community and within organizations both within and outside Baylor. I appreciate her leadership in these areas. She is able to provide new ideas or a different perspective to our team and that is welcomed. I appreciate that she is willing and open to continue to professional development opportunities. I appreciate that she is open to learning and open to feedback. An area of development would be to deliver the outcome to a project or investigation in a more timely manner.

Second-Level Manager Acknowledgement

Additional Comments

BFSA Letter of Recommendations (2019)

BLACK FACULTY & STAFF ASSOCIATION

September 4, 2019

To Whom It May Concern:

The Executive Committee of the Black Faculty and Staff Association (BFSA) at Baylor University, acting on behalf of its membership, comprised of full-time faculty, staff, and graduate students humbly submit this letter to share recommendations as they relate to diversity, equity, and inclusion at Baylor University. The Black Faculty & Staff Association (BFSA) has the capacity to assist the University in making advancements towards a more equitable Baylor in a way that will "embody Christ's teachings of love and inclusivity." As such, this letter will provide both suggestions and concerns that relate to matters of diversity and inclusion to support furthering the mission of the institution. We hope that the perspectives shared are both insightful and helpful.

Recruitment

It is evident that there have been positive and intentional efforts put forth in recruiting a diverse student population, but the intentional recruitment effort by both Human Resources and the Provost Office seems to lack the cultural competencies needed to hire Black faculty and staff. It is the recommendation of the BFSA that the University look more holistically at our recruiting efforts and forgo the expectation that this responsibility should reside solely with departmental chairs or recruiters. BFSA is poised to be a partner in the University's recruiting efforts by meeting with diverse faculty and staff candidates, helping to provide a sense of community and serving as a resource as they transition to Baylor and the Waco community.

Retention

As Baylor increases its ethnic diversity among its faculty, staff, and students, it becomes imperative that the University demonstrates its mission by promoting a welcoming and supportive community for those who may be from marginalized minority groups. How the University shows care for these family members may dictate whether potential faculty, staff and students make the decision to join the institution.

The BFSA recommends that Baylor develop intentional retention efforts for faculty and staff of color to reduce the amount of turnover experienced across the University. The departure of faculty and staff of color can directly impact the retention of our students. Research has shown that student retention rates increase as they become more connected to the institution. Black faculty and staff serve as mentors for students and help them to matriculate to graduation. These relationships help to increase a student's connection to the institution even after graduation. They may consider our post-graduate educational opportunities, as well as, become an engaged alumnus and financial contributor to the University. Currently there are only 31 Black faculty (3%) and 933 White faculty. While diversity reaches beyond race/ethnicity, those characteristics have an impact on students. The BFSA is interested and prepared to be a part of the strategic planning and dialogue on retention of faculty, staff, and students.

Climate Survey

BRITTNEY WARDLAW, J.D.

In the Spring 2017 semester, the former President's Advisory Council on Diversity assessed the climate of Baylor as it relates to diversity. Even though Dr. Livingstone released the results of the survey, there do not appear to be any tangible outcomes addressed by survey results. While we are aware that another climate survey is forthcoming, it is the recommendation of the BFSA that a plan of action is communicated to the faculty, staff, and student body as a response to the original survey. The plan of action can include a notification about the upcoming survey and proposed plans that can be used in the survey questions to ascertain if the proposed plan has the support of the University community. Moving forward, there would likely be more University participation if the Baylor community believes that their responses will be intentionally considered and positive change may result. After the completion of the new survey, BFSA recommends that a plan be proposed in a timely fashion to address the key findings of the survey.

Baylor Black Administrators

The percentage of Black faculty and staff members represented among the entire body of professionals at the University is extremely low. Dr. Dwayne Simmons and Dr. Mia Moody-Ramirez are the only Black department chairs while Pearlie Beverly, Tonya Hudson, and very recently, Dominque Hill, are the only Black departmental directors. As the Sr. Associate Athletic Director, Marcus Sedberry is the highest-ranking Black staff person at the University. It is the recommendation of the BFSA that the University become more intentional about developing, recruiting, promoting, and hiring Black faculty and staff.

Mentoring: Executive Cabinet

Currently, there are very few people of color represented on the President's Executive Cabinet. This lack of diversity has the potential to negatively impact the ability of the president to make informed decisions as they relate to Baylor's diverse student body. It is the recommendation of the BFSA that members of the President's Council serve as mentors to either faculty or staff of color in order to increase the capabilities, skills, and knowledge of aspiring administrators. It is important that the leadership not only communicate their support of diversity initiatives through written and verbal gestures, but also through the selection of high-profile administrators of color. Baylor should be intentional about creating spaces, mechanisms, and opportunities that produce the infrastructure for a more equitable environment. Mentoring has the ability to accomplish such an ideal.

Conclusion

The BFSA was founded in order to serve our historic institution. It is our hope that this letter will provide the administration with new perspectives concerning matters that affect a part of the Baylor Family that is often marginalized. *The BFSA welcomes the opportunity to discuss these recommendations and serve as a partner in order to provide support for the development of innovative initiatives.* Thank you for reviewing this letter.

Humbly Submitted,
Dominque Hill, President   Geoffrey Griggs, Treasurer
Brittney Wardlaw, President Elect Erica Johnson, Parliamentarian
Gretel Hill, Secretary   Tonya Hudson, Communications and Outreach Director

My Steps For HEALing: I'm Leaving BAYLOR (2020)

Brittney Deanne Wardlaw is with G.P. Wardlaw.
Jun 30, 2020

My Steps For HEALing: I'm Leaving BAYLOR

(JD, Former Deputy Title IX Coordinator & Former Manager of Equity & Civil Rights speaks out)

Two months ago, I started down a road that I knew would be irreversible. I made a decision to tell my untold stories of my three-year tenure at Baylor University. It began with a letter to the President on May 20, 2020 articulating my experience as a Black Woman working as an administrator in a two-person Equity office. I referenced how I was "systematically force(d)...to resign" the more I spoke up and out against the oppressive, dismissive, and minimized status of Black Faculty, Staff, and Students at the institution. The more I spoke up, the more difficult things got for me. I endured daily in hopeful expectation that my hard work, reputation, and credentials would proceed me. However, what proceeded me was the culture, and the concerning reputation of the university that has a history of suppressing the voice of many marginalized populations.

One of the many silenced voices has been that of the Black community. I have watched as staff members with little to no recourse are demoted and terminated for their failure to conform to a white culture; faculty members working twice as hard to receive tenure and mentor countless black students only to be told that they have not done enough work or research to be on track to receive tenure; I have watched as black students have made fruitless appeals to communicate their concerns of their professors' biases resulting in grades that prohibit them from graduating only to be told that the grading was completely fair.

Are black people being physically murdered at Baylor University? No. Are they being murdered professionally? Absolutely yes. Are they being murdered psychologically? Absolutely yes. Are they being murdered emotionally? Absolutely yes.

 **Brittney Deanne Wardlaw** is with **G.P. Wardlaw.**
Jun 30, 2020 ·

After being recruited to Baylor University, in 2017 I was murdered professionally when I agreed to move my family across the country to be the Deputy Title IX Coordinator, only to be demoted within five months after returning from unpaid maternity leave. I was murdered psychologically in 2018-2019 when I received consecutive positive performance reviews only to be denied five times for a promotion in hopes that I would reclaim a professional level of which I was qualified to occupy. I was murdered emotionally in 2020 when I was "insourced" to a student worker position and told I was "difficult to work with," that I "create obstacles," and that my work and ideas are too "visionary and forward thinking" and "that's just not where the University wants to go at this time."

As the former President-Elect of the Black Faculty & Staff Association (BFSA), the only Employee Resource Group at Baylor University, I was and still am hopeful that they will do some awesome work for the institution in moving toward change. There are many people and organizations like BFSA, that if supported by the institution, they can help bring about tangible change.

Two months ago, I started down a road to negotiate with Baylor for a severance agreement for my silence. After a very unsuccessful mediation (which I am so grateful for), I'm done being silenced. I've wanted nothing more than to be a positive contributor to help Baylor be the light that they claim to be. There are countless individuals with stories to tell who are not a in a position to be able to speak up.

I think it was Emmanuel Acho who said it best, that its not just the boat of slavery that impacts blacks in America, but the wake of that boat that has rippling and ongoing effects. But my husband and I have resolved that our mental health practice and platform "The Relationship Clinic of Waco" is committed to serving any and all who are interested in learning, growing, and ultimately HEALing from systemic racism by using the framework "i pray. i talk. i see a therapist." Whether an individual or an organization,

Brittney Deanne Wardlaw is with **G.P. Wardlaw**.
Jun 30, 2020

There has to be a point where we decide and admit that there's an ongoing problem and then commit to doing better. We are committed to those partnerships. No longer will we fight to convince anyone. We will instead focus our efforts on helping to HEAL from the wake and trauma of our racist histories.

I recognize that this decision to resign and speak out will leave me with attorney's fees and no severance agreement support. As a dear friend shared with me, "as I press and move forward, the wind at my back is the TRUTH that [the Lord] is PROUD OF [ME]," I am confident that He will provide for us. But I believe that the sacrifices made are worth it if it will help reconcile Baylor with the ongoing and present day effects of its racist past and give the Black Faculty, Staff, and Students and true allies a sturdier platform to have open and honest dialogue about how the institution can truly move forward in a genuine and palpable way.

#Baylor #BUrememberwhen #BeBetterBaylor #LiftBlackVoices #BU #newchapter #HEAL #TRC #TheRelationshipClinic #iprayitalkiseeatherapist #BWconsulting #freeatlast

WACOAN KWTX News 10 Waco Tribune-Herald The Dallas Morning News Houston Chronicle ABC News KWKT FOX 44 Los Angeles TimesCBS News

Insights unavailable   Boost a post

👍 Like   💬 Comment   🔗 Copy   ↗ Share

DJ Felder and 461 others

186 shares

www.ingramcontent.com/pod-product-compliance
Lightning Source LLC
Chambersburg PA
CBHW050859240426
43673CB00033B/496/J